Celebrating
the Mass

A Guided Discovery for Groups and Individuals

Kevin Perrotta

LOYOLAPRESS.

CHICAGO

LOYOLAPRESS.

3441 N. ASHLAND AVENUE
CHICAGO, ILLINOIS 60657
(800) 621-1008
WWW.LOYOLAPRESS.ORG

Nihil Obstat	*Imprimatur*
Reverend John G. Lodge, S.S.L., S.T.D.	Most Reverend Raymond E. Guedert, M.A., S.T.L., J.C.L.
Censor Deputatus	Vicar General
October 20, 2004	Archdiocese of Chicago
	November 10, 2004

The *Nihil Obstat* and *Imprimatur* are official declarations that a book is free of doctrinal and moral error. No implication is contained therein that those who have granted the *Nihil Obstat* and *Imprimatur* agree with the content, opinions, or statements expressed. Nor do they assume any legal responsibility associated with publication.

Except where noted, the Scripture quotations contained herein are from the New Revised Standard Version Bible: Catholic Edition, copyright © 1993 and 1989 by the Division of Christian Education of the National Council of the Churches of Christ in the U.S.A. Used by permission. All rights reserved. Subheadings in Scripture quotations have been added by the author.

Scripture quotation from the Revised Standard Version of the Bible, copyright © 1946, 1952, and 1971 by the Divison of Christian Education of the National Council of the Churches of Christ in the U.S.A. Used by permission. All rights reserved.

The excerpt from St. Alphonsus Liguori, p. 36, is taken from *The Practice of the Love of Jesus Christ,* Peter Heinegg, trans. (Liguori, MO: Liguori Publications, 1997), 13–14.

The excerpt from Romano Guardini, p. 37, is taken from *Preparing Yourself for Mass* (Manchester, NH: Sophia Institute Press, 1993), 27–28; reprinted with permission of Sophia Institute Press.

The excerpts from St. Catherine of Siena, p. 77, are adapted from *The Dialogue of the Seraphic Virgin Catherine of Siena,* Algar Thorold, trans. (New York: Benziger Brothers, 1925), 218–221, 224.

The quotations from the Congregation for Divine Worship, p. 91, may be found in "Holy Communion and Worship of the Eucharist outside Mass," *The Rites,* 2 vols. (New York: Pueblo Publishing, 1976), 1:484.

Throughout this book, excerpts from the Roman liturgy are from the English translation of *The Roman Missal* © 1973, International Committee on English in the Liturgy, Inc. All rights reserved. Excerpts from the Byzantine liturgy are from the translation used by the Eparchy of Parma, Ohio, as approved by the Congregation for Oriental Churches, 10 December 1964. The excerpt from the West Syrian liturgy was supplied by Our Lady of Deliverance Syriac Catholic Diocese in the United States and Canada, Union City, New Jersey.

Interior design by Kay Hartmann/Communique Design
Illustration by Anni Betts

ISBN 0-8294-2064-9

Printed in the United States of America
05 06 07 08 09 10 Bang 10 9 8 7 6 5 4 3 2 1

Contents

4   *How to Use This Guide*

6   *This Thing We Do*

14   **Week 1**
Standing among Angels and Saints
Psalm 65; Ephesians 2

26   **Week 2**
Listen! Remember!
Psalm 81 and Selections from Exodus 12–13

38   **Week 3**
Thanks and Praise Are Just Right
Selections from Psalm 136, Deuteronomy 26,
and Revelation 4–5

50   *Sacrifice, Offering, Gift of Self*

52   **Week 4**
The Perfect Offering
Selections from Exodus 24, Leviticus 16,
Luke 22, and Hebrews 9

66   **Week 5**
Happy Those Called to This Supper
Selections from Luke 24, Psalm 36, and
Revelation 19

78   **Week 6**
Going Out with a Blessing
Selections from Numbers 6, Luke 2, and
Romans 12

92   *Suggestions for Bible Discussion Groups*

95   *Suggestions for Individuals*

96   *Resources*

How to Use This Guide

If you want to understand why we celebrate the Mass, the natural place to begin is the Bible.

In this book we will read from Scripture to learn about the Mass. As we proceed, we will explore connections between what we find in Scripture and our own lives.

Our approach will be a *guided discovery.* It will be *guided* because we all need support in understanding Scripture and reflecting on what it means for our lives. Scripture was written to be understood and applied in the community of faith, so we read the Bible *for* ourselves but not *by* ourselves. Even if we are reading alone rather than in a group, we need resources that help us grow in understanding. Our approach is also one of *discovery,* because each of us needs to encounter Scripture for ourselves and consider its meaning for our life. No one can do this for us.

This book is designed to give you both guidance for understanding and tools for discovery.

The introduction on page 6 will guide your reading by providing background material and helping you get oriented to the subject of our exploration. Each week, a brief "Background" section will give you context for the reading, and the "Exploring the Theme" section that follows the reading will bring out the meaning of the Scripture passages. Supplementary material between sessions will offer further resources for understanding.

The main tool for discovery is the "Questions for Reflection and Discussion" section in each session. The first questions in this section are designed to spur you to notice things in the text, sharpen your powers of observation, and read for comprehension. Other questions suggest ways to compare the people, situations, and experiences in the biblical texts with your own life and the world today—an important step toward grasping what God is saying to you through the Scripture and what your response might be. Choose the questions you think will work best for you. Preparing to answer all the questions ahead of time is highly recommended.

We suggest that you pay particular attention to the final question each week, labeled "Focus Question." This question points to an especially important issue about the Mass raised by the reading. You may find it difficult to answer this focus question briefly. Do leave enough time for everyone in the group to discuss it!

Other sections encourage you to take an active approach to your Bible reading and discussion. At the start of each session, "Questions to Begin" will help you break the ice and start talk flowing. Often these questions are light and have only a slight connection to the reading. After each Scripture reading, there is a suggested time for a "First Impression." This gives you a chance to express a brief, initial, personal response to the text. Each session ends with a "Prayer to Close" that suggests a way of expressing your response to God.

How long are the discussion sessions? We've assumed you will have about an hour and twenty minutes. If you have less time, you'll find that most of the elements can be shortened somewhat.

Is homework necessary? You will get the most out of your discussions if you read the weekly material and prepare your answers to the questions in advance of each meeting. If participants are not able to prepare, read the "Exploring the Theme" sections aloud at the points where they appear.

What about leadership? You don't have to be an expert in the Bible to lead a discussion. Choose one or two people to act as discussion facilitators, and have everyone in the group read "Suggestions for Bible Discussion Groups" (page 92) before beginning.

Does everyone need a guide? a Bible? Everyone in the group will need their own copy of this book. It contains the biblical texts, so a Bible is not absolutely necessary—but each person will find it useful to have one. You should have at least one Bible on hand for your discussions. (See page 96 for recommendations.)

Before you begin, take a look at the suggestions for Bible discussion groups (page 92) or individuals (page 95).

This Thing We Do

"Do this in remembrance of me." Luke 22:19

It's spring. Looking ahead to summer, my son and his wife are hoping to have a barbecue with their children. Nothing fancy, probably some spareribs, potato salad, and soda on the patio behind the house. To Dominic, Heidi, and the children it won't seem ordinary, though. Dominic's an army doctor. Right now, he's deployed. On a Saturday afternoon some months from now, when, God willing, he's shooing the dogs away from the potato salad and giving the children one of his typically long answers to a short question while turning ribs on the grill, the very ordinariness of it all will seem far from ordinary. The fragrant curl of smoke, the familiar male voice, the usual scramble for seats at the picnic table—every detail will carry a weight of meaning: Dad is home; the family's together again.

If you think about it, what we do at Mass is fairly ordinary. There are no Olympic displays of endurance and skill; no blazing, computer-generated, video entertainments; just folks standing and sitting, reciting prayers and listening. We kneel, which is a bit unusual but requires no special training. Some of us sing, but the Metropolitan Opera we're not, or even the Grand Ole Opry. There is some walking back and forth and a little eating. Yet what an immense weight of meaning these simple actions bear!

In the Mass, Jesus Christ makes himself present to us. Consider who he is: the eternal wisdom through whom God brought all things into existence, the Word made flesh—God in human form. Jesus lived his whole human life in attentiveness to his heavenly Father; then he offered himself completely to the Father on a cross, rose in triumph over death, and reigns now in glory. In the Mass, Jesus gives us access to his giving of self, his death-conquering resurrection, his entry into God's presence in heaven. Jesus renews our relationship with him by making himself our food and drink.

The Mass, in a famous Catholic phrase, is the "source and summit of the Christian life." To participate in it is to get to the center of God's relationship with the human race and to expose ourselves to powers of personal transformation more profound than any others. In the Mass, God draws us into the life of his Son, making us "participants of the divine nature" (2 Peter 1:4).

Our low-key actions on a Sunday morning seem staggeringly out of proportion to the immensity of the unseen realities. Sometimes, as I look around at my fellow parishioners at Mass and think about what we're engaged in, I feel a bit dizzy—the way a passenger belowdecks might feel when his eyes tell him the cabin is level and steady, but his inner ear tells him the ship is pitching in a heavy sea.

The Mass is the source and summit of Christian life because it renews our contact with Jesus. If we wish to deepen our understanding of the Mass, the starting point is to ponder Jesus' role in God's plans. The primary source of insight into God's relationship with the human race is the Bible. The biblical story is long and complex, but its outline can be stated briefly. God created the human race intending that we would use our lives and the good things of earth to grow to maturity in companionship with him. We humans, however, chose a different path. Refusing to accept our lives with thankfulness to God and to live according to God's purposes, we preferred sin in various forms—selfishness, idolatry, injustice. God, however, did not accept our refusal as the end of the story. A prayer in the Mass summarizes the sweep of God's action:

You formed man in your own likeness
and set him over the whole world
to serve you, his creator,
and to rule over all creatures.
Even when he disobeyed you and lost your friendship
you did not abandon him to the power of death,
but helped all men to seek and find you.
Again and again you offered a covenant to man,
and through the prophets taught him to hope for salvation.
Father, you so loved the world
that in the fullness of time you sent your only Son to be our Savior.

He was conceived through the power of the Holy Spirit,
and born of the Virgin Mary,
a man like us in all things but sin.
To the poor he proclaimed the good news of salvation,

to prisoners, freedom,
and to those in sorrow, joy.
In fulfillment of your will
he gave himself up to death;
but by rising from the dead,
he destroyed death and restored life.
And that we might live no longer for ourselves but for him,
he sent the Holy Spirit from you, Father,
as his first gift to those who believe,
to complete his work on earth
and bring us the fullness of grace.

Eucharistic Prayer IV (Roman rite)

The statement "Again and again you offered a covenant to man, and through the prophets taught him to hope for salvation" refers to God's relationship with the people of Israel. "In the fullness of time" God sent his Son to become a man of this people, Israel. As a human being, living in ordinary circumstances and sharing our experience of suffering, Jesus did what no one else had ever done: he lived a perfect human life and died a perfect human death. While all the rest of us disobeyed God, Jesus obeyed. Rather than turning away from God's purposes, he offered himself to God for the fulfillment of God's intentions. In his self-offering to God, a mysterious transaction occurred. By his willing cooperation with God even in great suffering, by his trust in God even in the experience of abandonment at the cross, Jesus reversed our lack of cooperation with God, our lack of trust. Through his death in obedience to God, Jesus brought us forgiveness for our sins. Through his resurrection, he brought us the power of God's Spirit to help us in our moral weakness, the hope of resurrection in the midst of our mortality, the beginnings of the kingdom of God in our sin-ravaged world. It is this transaction that we celebrate in the Mass. As we celebrate, Jesus makes it present to us and draws us into it.

While God's plan can be summed up briefly, it is not easy to understand. In fact, the more one considers the matter, the more mysterious God's dealings with us seem to be. To begin, there is the mystery of why God, who needs nothing, wished to create anything in the first place and why, in particular, he wished to create us in his own "likeness." There is the mystery of the freedom he gave us to accept or reject his plans, and the mystery of his mercy when we chose to reject them. There is the mystery of God's Son becoming a human being and the mystery of the Son's death overcoming our death, of his faithfulness canceling out our unfaithfulness. Finally, there is the mystery of Jesus' risen life—and our sharing in it. While we may grow accustomed to talking about God, he remains far beyond our comprehension. God is *other* than everything we know in this world. He transcends our little minds. How, then, can God communicate with us? How can we arrive at some understanding of him?

Communication is possible because the universe that God has created, which we *can* understand to some degree, expresses God's grandeur, wisdom, and love. So God can use things in our world as metaphors for himself and his relationship with us. He can come down to our level, like an adult bending down to a child, and speak in terms we understand. He tells us that he is like a father—and a mother (Matthew 6:1–32; Psalm 131:2; Isaiah 42:14), like a lover (Song of Solomon 2:8–17), like a life-giving stream of water (Jeremiah 2:13), like a hostess or host at a banquet (Proverbs 9:1–6; Matthew 22:1–14), like a feast of rich foods (Isaiah 25:6). To explain God's kingdom, Jesus drew comparisons with familiar situations: it is like a shepherd leading sheep, like a woman baking bread, like a farmer sowing a field, like a poor woman searching her house for a single lost coin (Luke 15:3–7; Matthew 13:33; Matthew 13:1–9; Luke 15:8–10).

In addition to images and stories such as these, things and actions play a part in God's communications with us. In the history of Israel, God used places (such as the city of Jerusalem), buildings (the temple in Jerusalem), and ceremonies (sacrifices in the temple) to give people a sense of his holiness and accessibility, as well as provide them with opportunities to express their response to him.

Just as Jesus told parables to give his followers insights into God's kingdom, he prescribed actions to signify the coming of

God's kingdom to them. For example, he commissioned his disciples to immerse men and women in water as a way of showing that God is cleansing them from their sins (Matthew 28:19) and to anoint with oil as a means of showing that God's Spirit is bringing power and healing (Mark 6:7–13). Through these ceremonies, Jesus not only gives us an understanding of God's action; he does what is symbolized. Such ceremonies are called sacraments.

As the greatest sacrament, Jesus gave his followers a meal through which he would make his whole ministry, death, resurrection, and glory present to them. The original form of this meal was the Passover supper that Jesus ate with his disciples on the night before he died. In this meal Jesus used bread and wine—symbolic of nourishment and joy—to give himself to his disciples as the one who forgives sins and restores friendship with God.

As he gave his disciples the bread and wine at the Passover meal, Jesus told his disciples, "Do this in remembrance of me" (1 Corinthians 11:24). After his death and resurrection, they did exactly that. The Mass we celebrate today is the present form of that original meal. The Mass is essentially the Last Supper, celebrated in memory of Jesus. In this meal, our ordinary actions—standing and sitting, singing and listening, walking in procession and eating—become the means through which Jesus makes himself present, teaches us, and draws us into his life. As Jesus adapted the incomprehensible realities of the kingdom of God to our finite understanding by telling simple parables that anyone can grasp, he makes the realities of the kingdom present to our experience through simple activities in which all of us can participate.

While the Mass has a symbolic quality, it is not symbolic in the sense of reflecting absent realities, like a bouquet of roses that I might have delivered to my wife back home when I am away on a trip. By the Holy Spirit, the realities that are symbolized in the Mass are truly present. In the Mass, we are not engaging in a performance; we are interacting with Jesus Christ. We who gather to celebrate the Mass are not just his followers: we are truly members of his body. The entry procession with the Gospel book symbolizes Jesus' coming among us—and Jesus is really here! Taking up the gifts in the middle of the Mass does not merely signify offering ourselves to God; we are actually giving ourselves to God in union with Jesus. Jesus' death and resurrection are so truly present in our celebration that there is no difference between the altar on which the Mass is celebrated and the rock of Golgotha where Jesus died. The priest who leads the celebration is the living embodiment of Christ, speaking Christ's words, "This is my body . . . this is my blood . . ." (Matthew 26:26, 28). In the bread and wine, Jesus' action in the sacrament reaches a unique degree of reality: the bread and wine not only signify spiritual nourishment by Christ—they actually *become* Christ, body and blood, humanity and divinity.

Indeed, the reality of Christ's action in the Mass is so great that it might almost appear that he is the *only* one who is really acting in it. The Mass is Jesus teaching, offering, feeding, blessing. Yet the Mass is also very much something that we do. The very word *liturgy* that we apply to the Mass indicates this. *Liturgy* comes from a Greek word that contains the word for *work* and means "a public service." The Mass is our public service of praise and thanks to God. It is an activity in which all of us, priest and laypeople, work together, from beginning ("The Lord be with you." "And also with you.") to end ("Go in the peace of Christ." "Thanks be to God.").

Scripture is the word of God in the words of human beings. In a similar way, the Mass is Christ's action expressed in the action of the human participants. We gather for worship because he gathers us. We join in his prayer; by his Spirit he prays in us. As we listen to God's word, Christ shares with us his own attentiveness to the Father. We thank God for Christ's offering of himself for us; Christ offers himself and us to the Father. We remember Jesus' death and resurrection; he draws us into the life that he has opened up for us by his dying and rising.

The Bible is the source for understanding Jesus' role in God's plans. But is it also the source for understanding the Mass? After all, the Mass developed greatly after the biblical books were completed, around the end of the first century. Nevertheless, the Bible is essential for understanding the Mass, not only because it is our primary resource for knowing Jesus but also because it helps us understand the kinds of things that Jesus does and we do in the Mass—remembering, thanking, offering, blessing. In this book we will read selections from Scripture that illuminate these aspects of the Mass. The excerpts from Scripture will not explain everything that we pray and do in the Mass. But they will help us grasp the most important dimensions of this most important thing that we do.

In a general way, the sequence of themes in our scriptural readings will follow the sequence of events in the Mass:

◆ In Week 1 our readings speak about entering God's presence—a theme that corresponds to the introductory prayers in the Mass.

◆ In Week 2 our readings focus on listening to God and remembering what he has done—themes that have a particular connection with the Scripture readings and the sermon.

◆ The readings in Week 3, on praise and thanksgiving, lead us to think especially about the central prayer of the Mass, the eucharistic prayer, in which we solemnly thank God for Jesus' death and resurrection.

◆ The focus on the eucharistic prayer continues in Week 4, when our Scripture readings focus on Jesus offering himself for us to the Father.

◆ The biblical selections in Week 5, on feasting in God's presence, speak to us about Holy Communion.

◆ The readings for Week 6, which speak of blessing, relate especially to the conclusion of the Mass.

Yet, while these various themes stand out particularly at certain points in the Mass, all the themes characterize the liturgy as a whole. While we enter especially at the beginning, the entire Mass is an experience of entering deeper and deeper into God's presence. Throughout the Mass we listen to God and remember what he has done for us. From start to finish, the Mass is praise of God and a channel of his life-giving blessings. To discuss the themes, we must separate them and discuss them one at a time. But in the Mass, they are interwoven. All is entry, listening, remembering, offering, praising, blessing.

And not only do our themes extend through the whole Mass, they also converge. We praise God by remembering Christ's offering of himself to the Father. Our remembering of Christ's offering is our offering to the Father. And this offering is a sacrifice of praise.

It is possible to feel overwhelmed by the Mass. It is too much to take in all at once, or in a lifetime. I think of it as a white hole, that is, the opposite of a black hole. A black hole is a point in outer space possessing such enormous gravitational attraction that any matter or energy that comes near it is drawn into it and disappears. The Mass is a blindingly bright point of light from which all of God's love flares out. The eternal love of the Father for the Son and of the Son for the Father; the love of Father and Son for the human race; Jesus' incarnation, life, death, and resurrection; the gift of the Spirit; the kingdom of God—all stream toward us from the Mass. No human mind can ever make more than a beginning of understanding all that takes place in the Mass. But, with God's help, it is good to begin.

Glossary

Eucharist. A term for the Mass, coming from a Greek word meaning "thanksgiving."

Liturgy of the Word. The first half of the Mass, ending with the prayer of the faithful.

Liturgy of the Eucharist. The second half of the Mass, beginning with the offertory song and preparation of the gifts on the altar.

Eucharistic Prayer. The central prayer of the Liturgy of the Eucharist—and of the Mass as a whole. The eucharistic prayer begins with the priest's call to the people to "Lift up your hearts" and concludes with the priest's declaration to God, "Through him, with him, in him, in the unity of the Holy Spirit, all glory and honor is yours, almighty Father, for ever and ever." In the Roman rite there are four forms of the eucharistic prayer. See page 63.

Rite. The liturgical and spiritual tradition of a historical sector of the Church. Most Catholics follow the Roman rite. Other Catholics follow the Byzantine, Syrian, Armenian, or other rites.

STANDING AMONG ANGELS AND SAINTS

Questions to Begin

10 minutes
Use a question or two to get warmed up for the reading.

1   Where do you like to sit in church?

2   What was the biggest rainfall you've ever seen?

The grace of our Lord Jesus Christ and the love of God and the fellowship of the Holy Spirit be with you all.
—And also with you.

Opening Greeting (Roman rite)

Blessed is the kingdom of the Father and of the Son and of the Holy Spirit, now and ever, and forever.
—Amen.

Opening Prayer (Byzantine rite)

Opening the Bible

10 minutes
Read the passage aloud. Let individuals take turns reading the
verses of Psalm 65 and the paragraphs of the St. Paul's letter to
the Ephesians.

The Background

God is always and everywhere present, but often we do not pay
much attention to him. Arriving at church to celebrate the Mass is
a moment to collect our thoughts. Our Scripture readings this
week aid our reflection. In different ways, both speak about
entering God's presence.

Originally, Psalm 65 was a hymn for worship in the temple
of Jerusalem. As the priests went about their duties, the people
stood in the courtyard around the temple building and sang the
psalm, or perhaps listened as it was sung by a choir.

Writing to Christians in Ephesus, St. Paul speaks about
how God has acted through Jesus to bring us into his presence.
In fact, through Jesus, God has made us into the temple in which
he dwells. In the early Church, the distinction between Jewish
Christians and gentile Christians was on everyone's minds. Here Paul
speaks as a Jewish Christian to gentile Christians ("you" in verses
1–2, 11–13, 19), although he views Jewish and gentile Christians as
equal members of the one body of Christ (he speaks of both groups
when he says "us" and "our" in verses 3–7, 10, 14, 18).

The Reading: Psalm 65; Ephesians 2

Where Is Satisfaction Found?

Psalm 65:1 Praise is due to you,
　　　　O God, in Zion;
　　　and to you shall vows be performed,
　　2　　O you who answer prayer!
　　　To you all flesh shall come.
　　3 When deeds of iniquity overwhelm us,
　　　　you forgive our transgressions.
　　4 Happy are those whom you choose and bring near
　　　　to live in your courts.
　　　We shall be satisfied with the goodness of your house,
　　　　your holy temple.

5 By awesome deeds you answer us with deliverance,
    O God of our salvation;
  you are the hope of all the ends of the earth
    and of the farthest seas.
6 By your strength you established the mountains;
    you are girded with might.
7 You silence the roaring of the seas,
    the roaring of their waves,
    the tumult of the peoples.
8 Those who live at earth's farthest bounds are awed by
    by your signs;
  you make the gateways of the morning and the evening
    shout for joy.

9 You visit the earth and water it,
    you greatly enrich it;
  the river of God is full of water;
    you provide the people with grain,
    for so you have prepared it.
10 You water its furrows abundantly,
    settling its ridges,
  softening it with showers,
    and blessing its growth.
11 You crown the year with your bounty;
    your wagon tracks overflow with richness.
12 The pastures of the wilderness overflow,
    the hills gird themselves with joy,
13 the meadows clothe themselves with flocks,
    the valleys deck themselves with grain,
    they shout and sing together for joy.

We Share Jesus' Access to the Father

Ephesians 2:1 You were dead through the trespasses and sins 2 in which you once lived, following the course of this world, following the ruler of the power of the air, the spirit that is now at work among those who are disobedient. 3 All of us once lived among them in the passions of our flesh, following the desires of flesh and senses, and we were by nature children of wrath, like everyone else. 4 But God, who is rich in mercy, out of the great love with which he loved us [5] even when we were dead through our trespasses, made us alive together with Christ—by grace you have been saved—[6] and raised us up with him and seated us with him in the heavenly places in Christ Jesus, [7] so that in the ages to come he might show the immeasurable riches of his grace in kindness toward us in Christ Jesus. [8] For by grace you have been saved through faith, and this is not your own doing; it is the gift of God—[9] not the result of works, so that no one may boast. [10] For we are what he has made us, created in Christ Jesus for good works, which God prepared beforehand to be our way of life.

[11] So then, remember that at one time you Gentiles . . . [12] . . . were . . . without Christ, being aliens from the commonwealth of Israel, and strangers to the covenants of promise, having no hope and without God in the world. [13] But now in Christ Jesus you who once were far off have been brought near by the blood of Christ. [14] For he is our peace; in his flesh he has made both groups into one and has broken down the dividing wall, that is, the hostility between us. [15] He has abolished the law with its commandments and ordinances, that he might create in himself one new humanity in place of the two, thus making peace, [16] and might reconcile both groups to God in one body through the cross, thus putting to death that hostility through it.

[17] So he came and proclaimed peace to you who were far off and peace to those who were near; [18] for through him both of us have access in one Spirit to the Father. [19] So then you are no longer strangers and aliens, but you are citizens with the saints and also members of the household of God, [20] built upon the foundation of the apostles and prophets, with Christ Jesus himself as the cornerstone. [21] In him the whole structure is joined together and grows into a holy temple in the Lord; [22] in whom you also are built together spiritually into a dwelling place for God.

First Impression

5 minutes
Briefly mention a question you have about the reading or one thing in it that surprised, impressed, delighted, or challenged you. No discussion! Just listen to one another's reactions.

Exploring the Theme

If participants have not read this section already, read it aloud. Otherwise go on to "Questions for Reflection and Discussion."

Psalm 65. A joyful yet awed hymn to the God who has created—and keeps creating—everything, this psalm reminds us who it is we worship at Mass.

The psalm singers acclaim God as the giver of everything that sustains life (65:9–13). Earthly blessings, however, are not all the singers want. They are happy to be praying in the courtyard that surrounds God's "holy temple" in Jerusalem (65:4) because here they are assured of God's presence. While God who has created all cannot be localized in any building, he does make himself accessible in a special way in the temple. "We shall be satisfied with the goodness of your house" (65:4), the psalm singers declare. It is God himself that they seek. They are more interested in the giver than his gifts.

The psalm singers know that people can enter God's presence only by his invitation and grace—only if he forgives our sins (65:3) and brings us near (65:4). Images of storm-tossed waves and rioting mobs flash through the singers' thoughts (65:7): they know that nature and society are filled with uncertainties and dangers, and they feel the need of God's protection. Only in the hands of the one who brings the sunrise each morning can we be secure in dark times.

In the Hebrew text, verses 9–13 may be taken either as a celebration of the fact that God brings forth life from the earth or as a petition asking him to bring forth life. Either way, the psalm acknowledges God as the source of life. Of course, we must work for our daily bread; but the results of our work, and even the talents and strength with which we labor, are God's gifts.

Ephesians 2:1–10. Psalm 65 speaks of our need for God's "deliverance" (65:5). Paul emphasizes our need for God's help against forces that would lead us to destruction. An evil spiritual power is at work in the world, trying to draw us away from God (Satan—2:2; Paul describes this mysterious spiritual entity in first-century terms that may seem strange to us). In addition, we ourselves have a dark side—theologians call it original sin—that weakens our defenses against temptation, drags us into selfish behavior, and deludes us about our failings (2:3). Consequently, we are estranged from God and end up suffering the effects of our sins—a condition that Paul describes as being "children of wrath" (2:3). Paul does not deny that there is a lot of good in human life; he simply points out that in the midst of the goodness, something has gone seriously wrong.

But quite unexpectedly, God has intervened in our situation (2:4–5). "By grace"—by God's graciousness—we have been saved (2:5, 8). This is pure gift. "Dead people cannot bring themselves back to life," New Testament scholar Ernest Best points out. "We can arrange neither to be born nor to be reborn."

God has sent help in the form of his Son. By becoming one of us, the Son of God has joined us in our dead-end situation and has experienced the worst that befalls us: death. But Jesus has risen from the dead, raising us up with himself and—this may come as a surprise to many of us—taking us along on his return to the glory of God. Thus, not only will we share in Jesus' resurrection when God's kingdom comes fully; in the meantime, we already share in Jesus' heavenly life. He has "seated" us with himself in heaven (2:6). Although we continue to live amid the realities of this world, now we are also with Jesus in God's presence. We continue on our earthly journey, yet have already entered our heavenly home.

To be seated with Christ (2:6) is to share in his conquest of evil. We can already begin to experience this victory over sin in our personal lives: "by grace you *have been saved* through faith," Paul declares (2:8, emphasis added). Paul unpacks the meaning of this statement by explaining that God has created us anew in Jesus and has prepared a path of good deeds for us to follow (2:10).

We could never have brought about this state of affairs by ourselves. It is God's gift. But we do have a crucial contribution to make to the process. We must respond to the opportunity God has opened up before us. Will we live the life that God makes possible? Will we walk on the path he has paved for us?

Paul realizes that it requires struggle to keep our footing on this path (4:25–5:20; 6:10–20). He is well aware that we live in a world where sin seems to continue unabated. He knows that for most of us, the process of getting free from our sins can be long and difficult. Nonetheless, he insists on the reality of what God has done. God *has* made us alive together with Christ and *has* raised us up with him and seated us with him in heaven.

Paul's vision of our situation as followers of Christ is breathtaking. And it is this situation that we celebrate in the Mass. As we gather in church to praise God, we are already, mysteriously, standing before him in heaven. Our lives are "hidden with Christ in God" (Colossians 3:3). The light of God's kingdom is already shining on us. In the Byzantine liturgy, the priest prays, "It is proper and just to sing hymns to you . . . for you brought us forth from nonexistence into being, and raised us up again when we had fallen, and left nothing undone, until you brought us to heaven and bestowed upon us your future kingdom." In the Mass we offer God thanks and praise not from a great distance but up close—closer than the psalm singers could ever have imagined.

Ephesians 2:11–22. In verses 1–10, Paul has spoken about our being brought near to God as individuals. Now he speaks about our being brought near to one another, of our being formed into a group of people belonging to God. In Paul's mind, being joined together in Christ is an essential part of what it means to be saved. Jesus has given his life so that he might raise us up *together* into God's presence. Naturally, each of us comes to Mass looking for the inspiration and help we need for our own lives; at the same time, we worship God as "one new humanity" in Christ (2:15).

Paul is deeply conscious of the distinction between Jews and gentiles produced by God's special favor to the Jews. But God has now overcome this distinction by calling both Jews and non-Jews to experience life in Christ. In Jesus, all human divisions are overcome—between nations, between ethnic groups, between social classes, between family members. By submitting to the death that all human beings experience, Jesus killed the hostility between Jew and Greek (2:16)—and among all other groups of people as well. Now all of us "have access in one Spirit to the Father" (2:18). It is as members of this universal group, which is

Christ's body, that we enter God's presence in the celebration of the Mass.

The psalm singers were glad to be in the temple because God made himself especially present there. Paul declares that the temple where God makes himself present is Christ. Since we are member's of Christ's body, *we* have become the "holy temple"; we are the place where the living God makes himself especially accessible (2:20–22).

Reflections. We come into God's presence at the beginning of Mass, but not only at the beginning. As the priest moves from the chair where he presides to the pulpit where he preaches to the altar where he makes the offering, the whole community enters more and more deeply into the presence of God "who is rich in mercy" (Ephesians 2:4).

In one sense, our entry is effortless. We come into God's presence because Jesus has brought us. We already stand among the angels and saints before God's throne. All we need to do is open our minds and hearts to him. Yet this opening of heart and mind requires some effort on our part. Again, a prayer from the Byzantine rite is apt: "Let us, who mystically represent the Cherubim, and sing the thrice-holy hymn to the life-creating Trinity, now set aside every earthly care, so that we may welcome the King of all, invisibly escorted by angelic hosts." As we celebrate the Mass, it is up to us to set aside earthly cares in order to give God thanks and praise. This does not mean forgetting our earthly needs and the needs of our world. It does mean leaving behind our usual "earth is all" mentality in order to turn our attention to God. In his goodness, "we shall be satisfied" (Psalm 65:4).

Questions for Reflection and Discussion

45 minutes
Choose questions according to your interest and time.

1 Put your imagination to work: What other images might you use to express the point that the psalmist makes in Psalm 65:6–7?

2 The psalmist addresses God as "you who answer prayer" (Psalm 65:2). What prayer are you especially glad that God answered? How does knowing God as one who answers prayer affect the way a person relates to him?

3 Reread Psalm 65:9–13. What area of your life would you like to see God "water" and make fruitful?

4 What has been your most joyful experience of worshiping God? Is your experience of participating in the Mass usually joyful?

5 Does it seem that the Christians in Ephesus had been baptized as infants or as adults?

6 Some people feel they can worship God just as well by walking alone along a lakeshore on a Sunday morning as by being in church with a bunch of strangers. What might Paul say to someone who feels this way?

7 What makes it hard for a person to focus on God when coming to Mass? What helps?

8 What part does the Mass play in your spiritual life? How do you experience the Mass as a source of grace?

9 For personal reflection: Is the mood of the psalm singers in Psalm 65:4 your mood when you go to Mass? If it isn't, is it still worthwhile going to Mass?

10 **Focus Question.** What ways of relating to one another at Mass express the fact that all are members of the body of Christ? What ways of relating to one another outside Mass express this reality? How does treating one another as members of the body of Christ affect our celebration of the Mass?

Prayer to Close

10 minutes
Use this approach—or create your own!

◆ Pray an Our Father together. Then let one person read Colossians 3:1–17 aloud. Pause for silent reflection on this question: What one point that Paul makes in this reading could I act on between now and the next time I'm at Mass, in order to be better prepared to enter into the celebration? Conclude together with a Glory to the Father.

Suggestion: Before the next time you are at Mass, read Psalm 65, Ephesians 2, or Colossians 3:1–17 again, and reflect on the meaning these words might have for your participation in the Mass.

Saints in the Making

Two World Youth Days, Two Masses

This section is a supplement for individual reading.

By Mark Giszczak

I remember being at Sunday Mass at World Youth Day in Rome in the year 2000. There were two million people from every nation on the globe. The pope was celebrating Mass with seven hundred bishops and five thousand priests. It was as if the whole Church were present. We had all journeyed from our homes to this field, this altar. Even though I had only met a handful of people in the crowd, I felt united with all of my brothers and sisters. During the Mass it was as if the boundaries of language and culture collapsed for the sacrifice at hand. I sensed my heart being caught up in the love of Christ and the love of his people. That day I came to understand "how good and pleasant it is when brothers dwell in unity!" (Psalm 133:1, RSV).

Two years later, at World Youth Day in Toronto, I arrived early in the day to stake out a spot near the front of the crowd. One of the young women in my group really wanted to attend Mass, but we weren't going to be able to until the next morning. She went into the crowd and found a priest who consented to say Mass, but he had no Mass kit. Not deterred, she went from group to group trying to find a Mass kit. She eventually found some people from the Philippines who lent her a Mass kit. It included a tiny bottle of wine and a chalice that might have held an ounce of liquid.

The priest turned a box upside down and put a white towel on top. Then he laid out the miniature Mass implements and put on his vestments. As my friends and I gathered around this little altar for the Mass, about twenty other people joined us, some of whom did not speak English. As the Mass began, I could sense the wonder of it all. We might look like fools to anyone who did not believe: a couple of dozen people staring intently at a cardboard box and a man in a robe. But we saw through the poverty of the situation into the brilliant light of Christ. When the time for the consecration came, we all dropped to our knees and recognized Jesus present in the sacrament. Jesus had come to Toronto.

LISTEN! REMEMBER!

Questions to Begin

10 minutes
Use a question or two to get warmed up for the reading.

1 What kinds of things are easy for you to remember? What's hard to remember?

2 What event in your life do you always remember when the date on which it occurred comes around each year?

The Word of the Lord.
—Thanks be to God.
Liturgy of the Word (Roman rite)
Listen with awe and purity to the message of the gospel of our
Lord Jesus Christ. . . .
—Make us worthy, O Lord our God.
Liturgy of the Word (West Syrian rite)

10 minutes
Read the passage aloud. Let individuals take turns reading paragraphs.

The Background

Listen! This is the key word in Psalm 81. Like our psalm last week, this one was probably composed for chanting in the Jerusalem temple. God reminds the people about what he did for them. For years, they had labored as government slaves in Egypt—reflected in the mention of "burden" and "basket" (81:6), allusions to menial labor at construction projects. But God rescued them. After he brought them out of Egypt, he tested their loyalty in the barren Sinai peninsula (81:7).

Remember! The reading from Exodus takes us back to the time when the Israelites were in Egypt. At the moment the reading begins, God has brought a series of misfortunes on Egypt to persuade the king to release the Israelites. Now the moment of their liberation is close. God gives them instructions for a special meal, which they are to eat on the night before their departure. After the meal, he will bring a final calamity on Egypt, and the king will let the Israelites go. Even as God gives instructions for the meal, he directs the Israelites to continue to eat it in future years as a way of remembering his action.

Both readings give us much to ponder with regard to the Mass, where listening and remembering play an important part. Not only in the Scripture readings and sermon but in the prayers and singing we have the opportunity to hear God speaking to us. And the entire celebration reminds us of Jesus' ministry of teaching and healing, and especially of his death and resurrection.

The Reading: Psalm 81 and Exodus 12:1, 14, 17, 21–27, 50–51; 13:3, 8–9

Sing—and Be Silent

> Psalm 81:1 Sing aloud to God our strength;
> shout for joy to the God of Jacob.
> 2 Raise a song, sound the tambourine,
> the sweet lyre with the harp.

3 Blow the trumpet at the new moon,
    at the full moon, on our festal day.
4 For it is a statute for Israel,
    an ordinance of the God of Jacob.
5 He made it a decree in Joseph,
    when he went out over the land of Egypt.

  I hear a voice I had not known:
6 "I relieved your shoulder of the burden;
    your hands were freed from the basket.
7 In distress you called, and I rescued you;
    I answered you in the secret place of thunder;
    I tested you at the waters of Meribah. . . .
8 Hear, O my people, while I admonish you;
    O Israel, if you would but listen to me!
9 There shall be no strange god among you;
    you shall not bow down to a foreign god.
10 I am the LORD your God,
    who brought you up out of the land of Egypt.
    Open your mouth wide and I will fill it.

11 "But my people did not listen to my voice;
    Israel would not submit to me.
12 So I gave them over to their stubborn hearts,
    to follow their own counsels.
13 O that my people would listen to me,
    that Israel would walk in my ways!
14 Then I would quickly subdue their enemies,
    and turn my hand against their foes.
15 Those who hate the LORD would cringe before him,
    and their doom would last forever.
16 I would feed you with the finest of the wheat,
    and with honey from the rock I would satisfy you."

Eat—and Remember

Exodus 12:1 The LORD said to Moses and Aaron in the land of
Egypt: . . . 14 This day shall be a day of remembrance for you. You

shall celebrate it as a festival to the LORD; throughout your generations you shall observe it as a perpetual ordinance. . . . [17] You shall observe the festival of unleavened bread, for on this very day I brought your companies out of the land of Egypt. . . .

[21] Then Moses called all the elders of Israel and said to them, "Go, select lambs for your families, and slaughter the passover lamb. [22] Take a bunch of hyssop, dip it in the blood that is in the basin, and touch the lintel and the two doorposts with the blood in the basin. None of you shall go outside the door of your house until morning. [23] For the LORD will pass through to strike down the Egyptians; when he sees the blood on the lintel and on the two doorposts, the LORD will pass over that door and will not allow the destroyer to enter your houses to strike you down. [24] You shall observe this rite as a perpetual ordinance for you and your children. [25] When you come to the land that the LORD will give you, as he has promised, you shall keep this observance. [26] And when your children ask you, 'What do you mean by this observance?' [27] you shall say, 'It is the passover sacrifice to the LORD, for he passed over the houses of the Israelites in Egypt, when he struck down the Egyptians but spared our houses.'" . . .

[50] All the Israelites did just as the LORD had commanded Moses and Aaron. [51] That very day the LORD brought the Israelites out of the land of Egypt, company by company. . . .

[13:3] Moses said to the people, "Remember this day on which you came out of Egypt, out of the house of slavery, because the LORD brought you out from there by strength of hand; no leavened bread shall be eaten. . . . [8] You shall tell your child on that day, 'It is because of what the LORD did for me when I came out of Egypt.' [9] It shall serve for you as a sign on your hand and as a reminder on your forehead, so that the teaching of the LORD may be on your lips; for with a strong hand the LORD brought you out of Egypt."

First Impression

5 minutes
Briefly mention a question you have about the reading or one thing in it that surprised, impressed, delighted, or challenged you. No discussion! Just listen to one another's reactions.

Exploring the Theme

If participants have not read this section already, read it aloud. Otherwise go on to "Questions for Reflection and Discussion."

Psalm 81. The psalmist begins by calling the people of Israel to give God noisy praise. They should go all out in thanking the Lord for his goodness to them (81:1–5). But suddenly the psalm takes a sober turn. God listened to the Israelites when they cried out for help in their enslavement in Egypt. Since then, however, they have not been listening to God. Praising God is fine, but it's no substitute for listening to him (81:6–10).

The kind of listening God is looking for involves more than hearing words. It means paying attention to his actions and learning from them. God has demonstrated to the Israelites that he is the giver of life and, therefore, deserves their complete commitment. Since God deserves their complete commitment, they should shut out the other forces and attractions that vie for their commitment—"strange" gods the psalmist calls them (81:9). Listening to God means keeping the first commandment: "I am the Lord your God, who brought you out of the land of Egypt, out of the house of slavery; you shall have no other gods before me" (Exodus 20:2–3).

The Israelites have not learned this lesson, so God has let them wander off into whatever troubles they may get themselves into. But now, as they gather for worship in the temple, God renews his appeal to them: Put me first! Their assembly is not just an opportunity for making music; it is a chance to remember who God is and refocus their lives on him.

The events about which God reminds his people (81:6–7) happened long ago. But as the people stand in the temple singing, God is present with them. The God who spoke long ago to their ancestors on their journey through the desert is speaking to them *now.* If only they would listen to him! Only those who focus their lives on God will fully experience his goodness (81:13–16).

Exodus 12–13. In preparation for the Israelites' exodus—their "going out"—from Egypt, God gives instructions, through their leader, Moses, for a meal they are to eat together. God tells Moses that every Israelite household is to select a lamb or goat, slaughter it, smear its blood on the jambs and lintel of their front door, then roast and eat the animal. The blood will mark their houses, so that they will escape when God strikes down the firstborn sons of Egypt—the final misfortune designed to pressure the Egyptians into releasing the Israelite slaves (12:2–13, 21–23). After the meal, events occur as God has predicted. That night, the firstborn sons throughout Egypt die; Pharaoh finally allows the Israelites to leave. Next morning, the Israelites depart en masse (12:28–51).

Interwoven with the instructions for the Israelites' last supper in Egypt are instructions for celebrating the meal in the future. "This day shall be a day of remembrance for you" (12:14). Called the Passover, it will be an annual reminder of God's rescuing them from slavery. ("This rite" and "this observance"—12:24, 25—refer to the meal, not to the sprinkling of blood.)

God has more in mind here than mere recollection. Remembering through the Passover meal will deepen the participants' relationship with God. It will be less a matter of recalling historical facts (as in "on this day in 1819 the poet Walt Whitman was born") than of reflecting on the relationship (as a husband might say on his wedding anniversary, "Honey, when I think back to our wedding, I'm more grateful than ever for our marriage").

Each generation will remember the Exodus as God's action *on their behalf.* Throughout the centuries, the Passover meal will give each member of the Israelite community the opportunity to affirm that God's action on that long-ago night in Egypt was for him or her as much as for those who were actually present. "It is the passover sacrifice to the Lord," they will say, "when he struck down the Egyptians but spared *our* houses" (12:27, emphasis added). During the meal, the father will explain to the children that they eat it "because of what the Lord did for *me* when *I* came out of Egypt" (13:8, emphasis added). No matter how far into the past the Exodus recedes, each later generation will recognize that God acted *for us.*

How can later generations make this claim? It is partly because they would not exist if God had not brought their ancestors out of Egypt. In this sense, every later generation benefits from God's action at the Exodus. But there is a deeper reason why every generation can affirm, "God did this for *us*": God continues to be with the community. The same God who revealed himself as rescuer and liberator at the Exodus accompanies the community today. The celebration reminds the community: this is how our God showed himself to be—and how he is for us now.

Reflections. In the Mass, as in Psalm 81, we begin by praising God (we usually begin with an entrance hymn; on Sundays and feast days we also pray the Gloria), then shift into listening mode as Scripture is read. No matter what the biblical selections for the particular day may be, they remind us that God has acted on our behalf. Implicitly or explicitly, God's word in Scripture and the sermon asks us: Have you paid attention to what God has done? Have you made God the center of your life? Or have you wandered off and done your own thing? Whatever our answers, God's message to us is right out of Psalm 81: "O that my people would listen to me. . . . I would feed you with the finest of the wheat, and with honey from the rock I would satisfy you" (81:13, 16). The wheat and the honey—and the rock—St. Jerome wrote, are Christ.

Like the Passover meal, the Mass is a meal of remembering. In fact, the Mass *is* the Passover meal, because the Mass is essentially Jesus' Last Supper, and that supper was the Passover meal. Just as God gave instructions to the Israelites the night before the Exodus to remember the event in the future by celebrating the Passover meal, Jesus instructed his disciples the night before he died to celebrate his final meal in the future as a memorial of his impending death and resurrection. "Do this in remembrance of me," he told them (1 Corinthians 11:24). The Mass is this memorial of Jesus—and not only when the priest speaks the words "This is my body . . . this is my blood . . ." but from beginning to end. The reading of the Gospel reminds us of Jesus' birth, his public life, his death and resurrection. The Creed is a remembering. Above all, the eucharistic prayer is a brief but crucial remembering of Jesus' final meal, his voluntary death, and his glorious resurrection.

Like the Passover meal, the Mass is not a lifeless monument to past events, because the events we remember are not locked away in the past. Certainly, Jesus' life, death, and resurrection took place twenty centuries ago. But in Jesus, these events are not over and done with. He took on human nature on a particular day near the beginning of the first century—but he remains fully human, as well as fully divine, forever. Some thirty years later, he offered himself to the Father on a cross outside Jerusalem on a particular Friday afternoon—but he will be for all eternity the Son who is given fully to his Father's will. Early on Sunday morning, he emerged from the tomb—and he reigns now with the Father in the glory of his resurrection. Jesus' incarnation, life, death, resurrection, and glory are fully present in him. And since he is present with us as we celebrate this meal in memory of him, his incarnation, life, death, resurrection, and glory are present to us. As we remember him in the Mass, Jesus shows us the love with which he lived, died, and rose for us. He gives us access anew to the forgiveness of sins and the light of God's kingdom that he opened up for us by his death and resurrection. He brings us before the Father (remember our reading from Ephesians last week) and enables us to share in his eternal song of thanks to the Father. Thus we enter into the realities we remember.

Jesus promised his disciples, "Where two or three are gathered in my name, I am there among them" (Matthew 18:20). In the Mass, above all, we gather in his name, and he is among us. As we remember that he sat at table with his friends, that he hung in crucifixion, that he rose from the dead, we are present at his table, at his cross, at his tomb. The altar before us is the place where he offers himself to the Father, the place where he triumphs over death, the place where he dines with us.

Questions for Reflection and Discussion

45 minutes
Choose questions according to your interest and time.

1 Why would God interrupt people's praise of him (Psalm 81:1–5) in order to speak to them about listening to him (Psalm 81:6–8)?

2 "O Israel, if you would but listen to me!" (Psalm 81:8). Does God want the Israelites to listen to a new message or to a message they have already heard?

3 What are some reasons why a person might stop listening to God? What can help a person begin listening again?

4 "Open your mouth wide and I will fill it" (Psalm 81:10). What is God saying to you here?

5 "Moses said to the people, 'Remember this day on which you came out of Egypt, out of the house of slavery'" (Exodus 13:3). Why such an emphasis on remembering the event? Do you think the Israelites would have forgotten it?

6 For what are you especially grateful to God? How often do you remember it? How does your remembering affect your life?

7 For personal reflection: What Egypt has God brought you out of? What goal, desire, personal relationship, or fear is a false god for you? What effects does it have on your life? Do you want to be free from it? What step is God calling you to take? How can you accept his help?

8 **Focus Question.** Identify a time when you were especially struck by something said at Mass—either in the Scripture readings, the sermon, or elsewhere. How often do you hear something in the Mass as God's word to you? What could you do to listen more carefully for God's word to you at Mass? How do you respond to God's word outside of Mass?

Prayer to Close

10 minutes
Use this approach—or create your own!

◆ Ask one participant to read aloud the following reflection by St. Alphonsus Liguori, an eighteenth-century Italian pastor and preacher.

Saint Bernardine of Siena says that people remember more vividly and hold more dear the signs of love shown them in death. So when they come to die, friends are accustomed to leave to the persons they have loved in this life some gift, a garment or a ring, in memory of their affection. But you, my Jesus, in leaving this world, what have you left us in memory of your love? Not a garment or a ring, of course, but your body, your blood, your soul, your divinity, your whole self, keeping nothing for yourself. "He gave you all," says Saint John Chrysostom: "He left nothing for himself."

Pause for silent reflection, and give an opportunity for brief prayers that anyone may wish to express. End with the following prayer.

Lord Jesus, help us to remember your love for us each day. May we desire nothing more than to love you in return.

A Living Tradition

The Importance of Really Being There

This section is a supplement for individual reading.

On the eve of World War II, Romano Guardini, a German priest, gave a series of short talks before Mass to fellow Germans about how to take part in the liturgy. Here is an excerpt on the subject of participating with complete attention.

In the relations between people—service, friendship, love—in everything that belongs to the sphere of man and his work, work is genuine only in the degree that the doer inwardly participates in it. Colloquial speech has several telling expressions for this: he is "completely absorbed" in his work, or: "His heart isn't in it." For I can do a thing, alone and unaided, and still put very little of myself into it. My body goes through motions and some mental activity is exerted but on the whole my mind is elsewhere—and the work proceeds accordingly. The nobler, the more difficult or important the task to be accomplished, the more completely I must give it my attention, earnestness, eagerness, and love, participating in it from the heart and with all the creative élan of the mind. That is composure: heart and mind concentrated on the here and now, not off on daydreams; it is being *all here*.

This is true of all action, but particularly true of that which concerns us here, the service performed before God. The Liturgy is based on the fact of God's presence in the church, and begins with man's response to that presence. This is how it differs from private prayer, which can take place anywhere, at home or in a street or field, Primarily—and this is decisive—liturgy means service in the holy place. It is a great mystery, God's presence in a place, and demands as a response that we appear before that presence. There is a beautiful expression for this in Italian: *faro atto di presenza* ("to perform the act of *being present*"). It is the beginning of everything. But one must be really present—with body, mind, and soul, with attention, reverence, and love. That is composure. Only he who is composed can have God's presence within him and appear before Him to respond to His outpouring grace with adoration and love.

From *Preparing Yourself for Mass*

Week 3

THANKS AND PRAISE ARE JUST RIGHT

Questions to Begin

10 minutes
Use a question or two to get warmed up for the reading.

1 When was the last time you thanked someone?

2 When was the last time someone thanked you?

Lift up your hearts.
—We lift them up to the Lord.
Let us give thanks to the Lord our God.
—It is right to give him thanks and praise.

Beginning of the Eucharistic Prayer (Roman rite)

Opening the Bible

10 minutes
Read the passage aloud. Let individuals take turns reading paragraphs.

The Background

Last week we focused our attention on listening to God and remembering what he has done for us. Listening and remembering are receiving. This week's readings turn our attention to our giving to God. A hymn of praise in the Jerusalem temple, instructions for Israelite farmers about how to thank God for their harvests, a vision of the heavenly praise of Father and Son—three very different selections showcase important features of praise and thanks in Scripture. They help us understand the thanks and praise that we give to God in the Mass.

The Reading: Psalm 136:1, 5–6, 10–16, 26; Deuteronomy 26:1–11; Revelation 4:6, 8–11; 5:6–12, 14

Three Ways of Thanks and Praise

Psalm 136:1 O give thanks to the LORD, for he is good,
   for his steadfast love endures forever. . . .
 ⁵ who by understanding made the heavens,
   for his steadfast love endures forever;
 ⁶ who spread out the earth on the waters,
   for his steadfast love endures forever; . . .
 ¹⁰ who struck Egypt through their firstborn,
   for his steadfast love endures forever;
 ¹¹ and brought Israel out from among them,
   for his steadfast love endures forever;
 ¹² with a strong hand and an outstretched arm,
   for his steadfast love endures forever;
 ¹³ who divided the Red Sea in two,
   for his steadfast love endures forever;
 ¹⁴ and made Israel pass through the midst of it,
   for his steadfast love endures forever;
 ¹⁵ but overthrew Pharaoh and his army in the Red Sea,
   for his steadfast love endures forever;
 ¹⁶ who led his people through the wilderness,
   for his steadfast love endures forever. . . .

26 O give thanks to the God of heaven,
for his steadfast love endures forever.

Deuteronomy 26:1 When you have come into the land that the LORD your
God is giving you as an inheritance to possess, and you possess it, and
settle in it, 2 you shall take some of the first of all the fruit of the
ground, which you harvest from the land that the LORD your God is
giving you, and you shall put it in a basket and go to the place that
the LORD your God will choose as a dwelling for his name. 3 You
shall go to the priest who is in office at that time, and say to him,
"Today I declare to the LORD your God that I have come into the
land that the LORD swore to our ancestors to give us."

4 When the priest takes the basket from your hand and sets it
down before the altar of the LORD your God, 5 you shall make this
response before the LORD your God: "A wandering Aramean was my
ancestor; he went down into Egypt and lived there as an alien, few in
number, and there he became a great nation, mighty and populous.
6 When the Egyptians treated us harshly and afflicted us, by imposing
hard labor on us, 7 we cried to the LORD, the God of our ancestors;
the LORD heard our voice and saw our affliction, our toil, and our
oppression. 8 The LORD brought us out of Egypt with a mighty hand
and an outstretched arm, with a terrifying display of power, and with
signs and wonders; 9 and he brought us into this place and gave us
this land, a land flowing with milk and honey. 10 So now I bring the
first of the fruit of the ground that you, O LORD, have given me."

You shall set it down before the LORD your God and bow down
before the LORD your God. 11 Then you, together with the Levites and
the aliens who reside among you, shall celebrate with all the bounty that
the LORD your God has given to you and to your house.

Revelation 4:6 . . . Around the throne, and on each side of the throne, are
four living creatures. . . . 8 . . . Day and night without ceasing they
sing,
"Holy, holy, holy,
the Lord God the Almighty,
who was and is and is to come."
9 And whenever the living creatures give glory and honor and thanks
to the one who is seated on the throne, who lives forever and ever,
10 the twenty-four elders fall before the one who is seated on the

throne and worship the one who lives forever and ever; they cast their crowns before the throne, singing,

> [11] "You are worthy, our Lord and God,
>> to receive glory and honor and power,
>> for you created all things,
>>> and by your will they existed and were created." . . .

[5:6] Then I saw between the throne and the four living creatures and among the elders a Lamb standing as if it had been slaughtered, having seven horns and seven eyes, which are the seven spirits of God sent out into all the earth. [7] He went and took the scroll from the right hand of the one who was seated on the throne. [8] When he had taken the scroll, the four living creatures and the twenty-four elders fell before the Lamb, each holding a harp and golden bowls full of incense, which are the prayers of the saints. [9] They sing a new song:

> [11] "You are worthy to take the scroll
>> and to open its seals,
>> for you were slaughtered and by your blood you ransomed for God
>>> saints from every tribe and language and people and nation;
>> [10] you have made them to be a kingdom and priests serving our God,
>>> and they will reign on earth."

[11] Then I looked, and I heard the voice of many angels surrounding the throne and the living creatures and the elders; they numbered myriads of myriads and thousands of thousands, [12] singing with full voice,

> "Worthy is the Lamb that was slaughtered
>> to receive power and wealth and wisdom and might
>> and honor and glory and blessing!" . . .

[14] And the four living creatures said, "Amen!" And the elders fell down and worshiped.

First Impression

5 minutes
Briefly mention a question you have about the reading or one thing in it that surprised, impressed, delighted, or challenged you. No discussion! Just listen to one another's reactions.

Exploring the Theme

If participants have not read this section already, read it aloud. Otherwise go on to "Questions for Reflection and Discussion."

Psalm 136. The psalm singers praise God not by listing his attributes ("You are wise, mighty, faithful . . .") but by pointing to his actions. Deed by deed, they recount how God has *shown* his wisdom, power, and goodness. From their repeated refrain, the singers seem pretty enthusiastic: they don't get tired of recalling God's rescues and blessings. Their lengthy list gives the sense of an unlimited series of marvelous things God has done. Apparently the singers could go on indefinitely without running out of divine acts to mention (compare John 21:25).

Deuteronomy 26:1–11. In this harvest ceremony, the Israelite farmer brings some of his produce to a shrine as a token of thanks to God for bringing the Israelites into the land (26:3–10). The farmer recalls that his distant ancestors were migrants who led an unsettled life, exposed to various dangers (26:5). But, our thankful farmer remembers, God reversed their situation, giving this small, endangered group of people security and making them numerous.

As in the Passover meal, the Israelite farmer affirms that God did these things for *us:* "we cried to the Lord" (26:7) and "the Lord brought us out of Egypt" (26:8). The farmer's declaration is an implicit act of faith: the God who cared for our people in the past, the farmer affirms, shepherds us now. The farmer's declaration also implies his own commitment to this people to whom God has shown kindness.

At the end of his prayer, the farmer shifts from speaking *about* God to speaking *to* him: "So now I bring the first of the fruit of the ground that you, O Lord, have given me" (26:10). The farmer acknowledges that what God has done for the community of Israel he has done for him, the farmer: "I bring . . . the fruit of the ground that you, O Lord, have given *me*" (26:10, emphasis added). While the farmer sees himself as a member of the community of Israel, he takes responsibility for his own relationship with God. "You, God, have been good to me," he says, "and I have come to thank you personally."

Notice that, as in Psalm 136, the farmer's way of expressing thanks is to declare what God has done. He honors the giver by proclaiming his unexpected, undeserved, and important gifts.

Revelation 4–5. The book of Revelation is loaded with strange but powerful symbols. Chapter 4 gives a stunning impression of God as the supreme authority over all that is. The scene, New Testament scholar Gregory Beale remarks, "emphasizes not merely God's sovereignty over creation but that all things have been created to serve his purposes and especially that he unswervingly accomplishes his will through all history without any possibility of being thwarted in the process. His people must trust in this fact so that, even when they experience suffering, they can rest assured that it has a redemptive purpose and is in accordance with his will."

At present, of course, there is a huge gap between the total acknowledgment of God in heaven symbolized in chapter 4 and the world as we know it. "May your will be done on earth as it is in heaven" is a petition yet to be fulfilled. Chapter 5 reveals God's plan for bringing the world into obedience to his will.

God's kingdom has entered the rebellious human world through his Son, Jesus. By portraying Jesus as a slaughtered lamb (5:6), John emphasizes that Jesus has begun to reestablish God's rule over human beings not by destroying and punishing but by laying down his life, not by force but by love. Jesus' submission to death was an act of apparent weakness, but by it he has conquered the power of sin in the world and has brought God's redeeming love to men and women. In the scene depicted in chapter 5, Jesus is praised for his victory as he enters heaven.

The heavenly chorus acclaims Jesus for making his followers priests (5:10). He has, in other words, empowered us to do what priests in the ancient world did—enter God's presence to offer thanks and praise. Still on earth, we already share with the heavenly beings in the worship of "the one seated on the throne" and of the "Lamb." As St. Paul put it in our reading in Week 1, we have been raised up and seated "in the heavenly places in Christ Jesus" (Ephesians 2:6).

Reflections. *What do we thank God for?* The psalm singers thank God for creating the earth and for taking care of his people. We see the same twofold praise in Deuteronomy, where the farmer thanks God for the fertile earth that God has created and for God's giving the farmer a corner of this earth to live on. Likewise, in John's vision of heaven, various creatures praise God for creating all things (Revelation 4) and praise Jesus for rescuing men and women from sin and death at the cost of his own life (Revelation 5).

In the Mass, also, we thank God for creation. In one prayer we pray: "Father, all-powerful and ever-living God, we do well always and everywhere to give you thanks. All things are of your making, all times and seasons obey your laws, but you chose to create man in your image, setting him over the whole world in all its wonder. You made man the steward of creation, to praise you day after day for the marvels of your wisdom and power, through Jesus Christ our Lord" (Preface V, Sundays in Ordinary Time, Roman rite).

Nevertheless, in the Mass the focus of our thanksgiving is on God's saving deeds, above all, the saving death and resurrection of his Son. Rather than thank God, as did the farmer of Deuteronomy, for leading us into a particular land, we thank God for leading us into his kingdom and letting us experience his presence.

How do we give thanks? In biblical Hebrew, the basic meaning of the word for *thank* is "acknowledge." It can be used for acknowledging bad as well as good. For example, the word is used for acknowledging, or confessing, one's sins (Psalm 32:5, "I will confess my transgressions"). Thus, as we see in Psalm 136 and Deuteronomy 26, people express thanks not by saying "thank you" (there was no such expression in biblical Hebrew) but by appreciatively declaring what the giver had given.

If you look closely, you will see that this is the basic approach to thanksgiving in the Mass, also. In the Mass we do a lot of acknowledging of what God has done for us. The hymns, the Scripture readings, the Creed—all declare God's deeds. In this way, the entire Mass is an act of thanksgiving, including parts, like the Creed, that do not explicitly speak of thanksgiving.

The core of our thanksgiving in the Mass is the eucharistic prayer. Here we acknowledge God's most profound act of love: the voluntary death and resurrection of his Son. In the Roman rite, the priest has several forms of the eucharistic prayer from which to choose. None of them contains a lengthy account of Jesus' life, death, and resurrection. But at the center of every one is a fragment of narrative: at the Last Supper, Jesus took bread, blessed and broke it, and gave it to his disciples, saying, "Take and eat. . . ." This brief recollection brings to mind the whole mystery of Jesus' becoming a human being for us, his life and teaching, his saving death and resurrection. This is God's supreme act of love for us. Recounting it, acknowledging it, is our supreme act of thanksgiving to God.

What happens when we give thanks? "You have no need of our praise," another prayer in the Mass declares, "yet our desire to thank you is itself your gift. Our prayer of thanksgiving adds nothing to your greatness, but makes us grow in your grace, through Jesus Christ our Lord" (Weekday Preface IV, Roman rite). Praising and thanking God turns us outward from ourselves and reminds us of God's awesome greatness and holiness. We recognize anew that everything is a gift from him, created to be an instrument of his love for us. Russian Orthodox theologian Alexander Schmemann writes: "Not giving thanks is the root and the driving force of that *pride* in which all teachers of the spiritual life . . . see the sin that tore man away from God." By reminding us of our complete dependence on God, thanksgiving sweeps away our pride, making room for God to reveal himself to us.

In Psalm 65 (Week 1), the psalm singers imagine the hills and valleys singing with joy to God (65:8, 12–13). But really, we praise God on their behalf. To stand in the presence of the life-creating God and acknowledge his goodness and love on behalf of all creation is to fulfill our highest call and deepest need.

Questions for Reflection and Discussion

45 minutes
Choose questions according to your interest and time.

1 Who is being addressed in Psalm 136:1 and 136:26?

2 From whose point of view were the events in Psalm 136:10 and 136:15 an expression of God's steadfast love?

3 Do you find the repetition in Psalm 136 tiresome? What is the place of repetition in prayer?

4 How often is the word *give* in various forms used in Deuteronomy 26:1–11? Who is the giver? What point does this repetition emphasize?

5 Besides words, what other expressions of praise are illustrated in these readings? (You might also look back to Psalms 65 and 81 in Weeks 1 and 2.) Which of these expressions are also found in the Mass? How might these Scripture passages help in understanding what we do in the Mass?

6 Compare the farmer's statement in Deuteronomy 26:1–11 to the Creed used in the Mass. How are they similar? How are they different? In what way is the Creed an expression of thanks to God? How might the farmer be a model for your own thanks to God?

7 Is it possible to give thanks to God in times of difficulty and loss? At such times, what is the importance of giving God thanks and praise through the Mass?

8 Before one can thank God for his deeds, one needs to know what he has done. In our lives and in the world today, how can one recognize God's activity?

9 What are you thankful to God for today? What will you especially thank God for next time you go to Mass?

10 **Focus Question.** How can giving God thanks in the Mass stimulate a person to give God thanks outside the Mass? How do you express your thanks to God outside of Mass? What opportunities do you have for thanking God by acknowledging to other people what he has done?

Prayer to Close

10 minutes
Use this approach—or create your own!

◆ Begin by praying Psalm 111. If
participants have different
translations, take turns reading
verses from each person's
translation. Then take a few
minutes for participants who
wish to pray brief thanksgivings
to God. End by praying the Our
Father together.

A Living Tradition

Offerings for God, the Clergy, and for the Poor

This section is a supplement for individual reading.

Did you notice, at the end of our reading from Deuteronomy about first fruits, that the thankful farmer has a feast with his family, the Levites (assistants who operate the shrine), and "aliens" (26:11)? Why invite strangers to the celebration? Scholar Jeffrey H. Tigay offers an explanation: "The farmer whose ancestors sojourned as strangers in Egypt and were oppressed, now provides generously for the strangers in his own land."

Deuteronomy also gives instructions about offering tithes, that is, tenths, of produce to God. The tithes are set aside for "the Levites, . . . the resident aliens, the orphans, and the widows" so that they may "come and eat their fill" (Deuteronomy 14:28–29).

These customs demonstrate a certain logic. We show thankfulness to God by giving back to him a portion of what he gives us, with prayer. The portion we return provides for those who serve us on God's behalf and for people who are in need.

In Rome, in early centuries when ordinary leavened bread was used in Holy Communion, the presentation of the gifts in the Mass dramatized this logic. Christians made bread at home and brought the loaves to church. After the Scripture readings and preaching, deacons went among the people to collect the loaves and arrange them on the altar. Loaves not needed for the Mass were stacked on nearby tables. The bishop then prayed a prayer over the bread and began the eucharistic prayer. After Mass, the deacons kept some of the extra loaves for the clergy and distributed the remainder to the poor.

Today, the presentation of bread and wine is a simpler affair: a handful of people bring the gifts up the aisle to the priest. These gifts are used solely for the celebration of the liturgy. At the same time, however, ushers take up a collection, which provides for the clergy and church, and on occasion is devoted also to charitable causes. Thus we continue to express the biblical logic of thanksgiving. We return some of God's gifts to him. Some of what we return supports those who work directly in the Church; some goes to meet our neighbors' needs. All that we give—both the tokens of bread and wine and the financial support—expresses our thanks to God for his goodness to us.

Between Discussions

Sacrifice, Offering, Gift of Self

The biblical readings in our next session speak about sacrifice. Before we begin these readings, it will be helpful to take a brief look at the subject in the Bible.

Some of our readings have already touched on the subject of sacrifice. Psalms 65 and 136 (Weeks 1 and 3), for example, may have been sung by choirs in the Jerusalem temple while the priests slaughtered animals and burned them on a large walk-up altar. The Passover lamb was a sacrifice (Exodus 12:27). The firstfruits that the Israelite farmer brought were a kind of sacrifice (Deuteronomy 26:1–11).

Other Old Testament sacrifices are mentioned in the Mass. One eucharistic prayer asks God to "look with favor on these offerings and accept them as once you accepted the gifts of your servant Abel, the sacrifice of Abraham, our father in faith, and the bread and wine offered by your priest Melchizedech" (Eucharistic Prayer I, Roman rite; see Genesis 4:4; 22:13; 14:17–20).

It is difficult to find a single concept that ties together all the various sacrifices in the Old Testament. But an underlying idea is suggested by some of the Hebrew words that are used. The most general expressions for sacrifice are forms of Hebrew words meaning "bring near," "send up," and "gift." Basically, a sacrifice is something that is brought to God, something sent up to him in smoke, a gift presented to him. The assumption, apparently, is that people should not only speak their gratitude or sorrow for sin but also show it with gifts.

Today we tend to associate the concept of sacrifice with suffering and death. But death is not necessarily involved in the Old Testament sacrifices because not all of them involve animals. Grain and oil are offered (Leviticus 2). Melchizedek offers bread and wine (Genesis 14:17–20). When animals are involved, they are slaughtered; but no significance is attributed to their pain.

To a greater or lesser degree, sacrificial gifts in the Old Testament signify the offerers' gift of themselves. Indeed, God makes it very clear that offering him sacrifice without giving one's self—one's heart, one's behavior—is a meaningless exercise, in fact, an insult (Isaiah 66:1–4; Hosea 6:6).

Particular types of sacrifice have distinctive meanings. Some are an expression of worship and acknowledge that God is the source of life and blessing (the kind of sacrifice that may have accompanied Psalm 65; Deuteronomy 12:6–7; 14:22–23, 28–29; 15:19–23). Some sacrifices express sorrow for sin and desire for reconciliation with God (Leviticus 4:1–6:7). Some give thanks for deliverance from sickness or danger (Leviticus 7:11–15).

Sacrifices that involve animals tend to focus on the ceremonial handling of their blood (Exodus 12–13; 24). This is because blood represents—in Israelite thinking, contains—life. As we are about to see, the rescuing-from-death effect of the Passover lamb's blood, the covenant-sealing blood of bulls in the ceremony ratifying the relationship between God and the people of Israel, and the sin-forgiving ritual with animals' blood by the high priest on the Day of Atonement all help to explain what Jesus accomplishes by his death on the cross. His death preserves our lives; it forgives our sins; it creates a deep bond between God and us.

While the Old Testament sacrifices help to explain what Jesus accomplished through his death, his self-offering transcends the Old Testament categories. Unlike the sacrifices of the Old Testament, Jesus offers not a token of himself—an animal or handful of grain—but himself. He sheds his own blood; he gives his own life. His sacrifice is not a ceremonial act but a real-life act of obedience to the Father (see Romans 5:17–19).

The biblical concept of sacrifice remains mysterious. Nowhere do the biblical writers explain how sacrifices work. The Old Testament authors present the sacrificial system as a gift from God, prescribed by him as a means by which his people can express their relationship with him and through which he promises to act in their lives. But the authors do not explain why sacrifice is a means by which God chooses to work. Jesus provides no explanation for why his suffering and death were essential to God's saving plan. In Luke's Gospel, he simply declares that it had to be (Luke 24:26). Nor do any of the New Testament authors explain how Jesus' death conquers death for us and brings forgiveness of our sins. They simply set Jesus' sacrifice of himself before us as the ultimate human gift to God, which brings life to the world.

THE PERFECT OFFERING

Questions to Begin

10 minutes
Use a question or two to get warmed up for the reading.

1   What cleaning tasks do you like? Which don't you like?

2   When you were a child, what was one place you were not allowed to go?

In memory of his death and resurrection, we offer you, Father, this life-giving bread, this saving cup.

Eucharistic Prayer II (Roman rite)

Remembering . . . all that was done in our behalf: the cross, the tomb, the resurrection on the third day, the ascension into heaven, the sitting at the right hand, the second and glorious coming again: We offer to you yours of your own, in behalf of all and for all.

Eucharistic Prayer (Byzantine rite)

Opening the Bible

4

10 minutes
*Read the passage aloud. Let individuals take turns reading
paragraphs.*

The Background

As our first reading begins, God has brought the Israelites safely
out of Egypt and has given them instructions for the way of life he
wishes them to follow. Now they commit themselves to the
covenant that God is offering them. In our second reading, God
gives directions for an annual feast, called the Day of Atonement,
on which the people's sins will be purged away through sacrificial
ceremonies. In our two New Testament readings, Jesus and the
author of the letter to the Hebrews use these Old Testament texts
to show that Jesus' death is a sacrifice that forgives sins and
forges a new covenant between us and God.

These readings bring us to the heart of the Mass. In a
mysterious way, Jesus' sacrificial death is present in the Mass. Jesus
offers himself to God; by remembering his offering, we offer him and
ourselves with him. This is the greatest act of praise and thanks to
God. Here all the themes of our previous readings converge.

The Reading: Exodus 24:3–8; Leviticus 16:2–3, 11–16; Luke 22:14–20; and Hebrews 9:11–15, 18–20, 22–26

A Covenant-Making Sacrifice

Exodus 24:3 Moses came and told the people all the words of the LORD
and all the ordinances; and all the people answered with one voice, and
said, "All the words that the LORD has spoken we will do." 4 And
Moses wrote down all the words of the LORD. He rose early in the
morning, and built an altar at the foot of the mountain, and set up
twelve pillars, corresponding to the twelve tribes of Israel. 5 He sent
young men of the people of Israel, who offered burnt offerings and
sacrificed oxen as offerings of well-being to the LORD. 6 Moses took
half of the blood and put it in basins, and half of the blood he dashed
against the altar. 7 Then he took the book of the covenant, and read it
in the hearing of the people; and they said, "All that the LORD has
spoken we will do, and we will be obedient." 8 Moses took the blood
and dashed it on the people, and said, "See the blood of the covenant
that the LORD has made with you in accordance with all these words."

A Sacrifice for Removing Sins

Leviticus 16:2 The LORD said to Moses:

Tell your brother Aaron not to come just at any time into the sanctuary inside the curtain before the mercy seat that is upon the ark, or he will die; for I appear in the cloud upon the mercy seat. 3 Thus shall Aaron come into the holy place: with a young bull for a sin offering and a ram for a burnt offering. . . .

11 Aaron shall present the bull as a sin offering for himself, and shall make atonement for himself and for his house; he shall slaughter the bull as a sin offering for himself. 12 He shall take a censer full of coals of fire from the altar before the LORD, and two handfuls of crushed sweet incense, and he shall bring it inside the curtain 13 and put the incense on the fire before the LORD, that the cloud of the incense may cover the mercy seat that is upon the covenant, or he will die. 14 He shall take some of the blood of the bull, and sprinkle it with his finger on the front of the mercy seat. . . .

15 He shall slaughter the goat of the sin offering that is for the people and bring its blood inside the curtain, and do with its blood as he did with the blood of the bull, sprinkling it upon the mercy seat and before the mercy seat. 16 Thus he shall make atonement for the sanctuary, because of the uncleannesses of the people of Israel, and because of their transgressions, all their sins. . . .

This Death, Too, Will Be a Sacrifice

Luke 22:14 When the hour came, he took his place at the table, and the apostles with him. 15 He said to them, "I have eagerly desired to eat this Passover with you before I suffer; 16 for I tell you, I will not eat it until it is fulfilled in the kingdom of God." 17 Then he took a cup, and after giving thanks he said, "Take this and divide it among yourselves; 18 for I tell you that from now on I will not drink of the fruit of the vine until the kingdom of God comes." 19 Then he took a loaf of bread, and when he had given thanks, he broke it and gave it to them, saying, "This is my body, which is given for you. Do this in remembrance of me." 20 And he did the same with the cup after supper, saying, "This cup that is poured out for you is the new covenant in my blood."

A Sacrifice Forgiving Sins and Making a New Covenant

Hebrews 9:11 ... When Christ came as a high priest of the good things that have come, then through the greater and perfect tent (not made with hands, that is, not of this creation), 12 he entered once for all into the Holy Place, not with the blood of goats and calves, but with his own blood, thus obtaining eternal redemption. 13 For if the blood of goats and bulls ... sanctifies those who have been defiled so that their flesh is purified, 14 how much more will the blood of Christ, who through the eternal Spirit offered himself without blemish to God, purify our conscience from dead works to worship the living God!

15 For this reason he is the mediator of a new covenant, so that those who are called may receive the promised eternal inheritance, because a death has occurred that redeems them from the transgressions under the first covenant.... 18 Hence not even the first covenant was inaugurated without blood. 19 For when every commandment had been told to all the people by Moses in accordance with the law, he took the blood of calves and goats ... and sprinkled both the scroll itself and all the people, 20 saying, "This is the blood of the covenant that God has ordained for you." ... 22 Indeed, under the law almost everything is purified with blood, and without the shedding of blood there is no forgiveness of sins.

23 Thus it was necessary for the sketches of the heavenly things to be purified with these rites, but the heavenly things themselves need better sacrifices than these. 24 For Christ did not enter a sanctuary made by human hands, a mere copy of the true one, but he entered into heaven itself, now to appear in the presence of God on our behalf. 25 Nor was it to offer himself again and again, as the high priest enters the Holy Place year after year with blood that is not his own; 26 ... But as it is, he has appeared once for all at the end of the age to remove sin by the sacrifice of himself.

First Impression

*5 minutes
Briefly mention a question you have about the reading or one thing in it that surprised, impressed, delighted, or challenged you. No discussion! Just listen to one another's reactions.*

Exploring the Theme

If participants have not read this section already, read it aloud.
Otherwise go on to "Questions for Reflection and Discussion."

Exodus 24:3–8. After liberating the Israelites from Egypt, God has led them into the barren Sinai peninsula and given them instructions for a way of life. Are the people willing to follow it? If so, the moment has come to ratify their relationship, their covenant, with God. The ceremony follows ancient Near Eastern custom, with a review of responsibilities, an oath of loyalty, and a sacrifice. The altar represents God; the twelve pillars, the people. Bulls are slaughtered (eighty-year-old Moses lets the young men do the heavy lifting). The people promise to carry out God's instructions faithfully. Then Moses splashes the bulls' blood on the altar and on the people—or perhaps on the pillars. The practice of sloshing around animals' blood may strike us as odd, but the meaning is not obscure: splashed with the blood of the same animals, God and the people are bonded in a relationship of total mutual commitment.

 Leviticus 16. Here we read a few instructions for the complex ceremonies on the annual Day of Atonement. The setting for the priest's activity is a tent shrine standing at the center of the Israelites' camp in the Sinai wilderness, symbolizing God's presence in the midst of the people. God makes himself especially present in the innermost part of the shrine (16:2, 16; the "sanctuary," elsewhere in the Bible called the Holy of holies). There a wooden chest containing the stone tablets with the Ten Commandments is kept. Over this chest (called the Ark of the Covenant) is an elaborately carved lid, here called "the mercy seat" (16:2, 13–15). On the feast, the high priest parts the curtain and enters the inner chamber. The incense cloud that he sends up in front of him (16:12–13) is a symbolic shield against the intensity of God's presence. It is an awesome thing to approach the living God!

 In the mentality that lies behind the ceremony, the people's sins are thought of as pollutants that adhere to the mercy seat and the sanctuary. The animals' blood is a ceremonial detergent that purges away these accumulated impurities (16:16). The Hebrew word for "make atonement" (16:11) means basically to rub off or wipe away. Ritually cleansing the sanctuary symbolizes God's cleansing the people of their sins (16:16). The ceremony is a sacramental kind of action, through which God forgives the people and grants them a fresh start in their relationship with him. The priest must carry out the prescribed actions to achieve atonement, but God forgives the people's sins. It is God, after all, who prescribes the ritual. The process is called *atone*ment because it makes the people *at one* with God.

Luke 22:14–20. More than a thousand years later, Jesus sits down to a Passover meal in Jerusalem. It is the night before his death. At several points during the Passover meal, the host at table customarily offers prayers that recall God's rescue of the Israelites from Egypt and ask for his continued aid. Jesus gives thanks also, apparently at the usual points in the meal; but rather than focusing on the Exodus from Egypt, he refers to his impending death (22:17, 19, 20). Instead of declaring, "This is the bread of affliction, which our fathers had to eat as they came out of Egypt," as might be said at the Passover meal, he gives the bread to his disciples with the declaration: "This is my body, which is given for you" (22:19).

The following day, when Jesus is crucified at Golgotha, many observers will regard him as a failure. His death will seem proof that he was totally misguided (Luke 23:35–38). But at his Last Supper, Jesus gives his disciples clues to help them see the reality behind the appearances. By linking his death with the Passover, Jesus indicates that his dying will create a new exodus—from the slavery of sin and death. By speaking of his body as "given," a word with sacrificial overtones, he implies that his death will be sacrificial: like the Passover lamb, he will be sacrificed to preserve men and women—in this case, to preserve us from the judgment that falls on sin. In his words over the cup, Jesus speaks of a "covenant" (22:20)—an allusion to the covenant-making sacrifice at Sinai (Exodus 24:3–8), indicating that his death also will be a covenant-making sacrifice. Jesus specifies that this covenant will be "new." Thus it will fulfill God's promise to draw us into a deep relationship with himself and give us a change of heart (Jeremiah 31:31–34; compare Ezekiel 36:24–27).

Hebrews 9:11–26. The author declares that Jesus has done in fact what the high priest did only symbolically. The high priest's entering the inner chamber of the tent shrine on the Day of Atonement was a symbolic entry into God's presence. Jesus has now literally entered God's presence in the "greater and perfect" sanctuary—"heaven itself" (9:11, 24).

Simultaneously, Jesus has entered our hearts, purifying us from our sins (9:14, 26; see Isaiah 57:15). Now that Jesus has cleansed our hearts, we can actually enter God's presence and worship him (9:14; 10:19–22; 12:22–24).

Rather than approaching God with a symbolic gift of animals' blood, Jesus has offered the real thing: himself (9:14, 25–26). By submitting to crucifixion, Jesus gave himself to God in an act of perfect obedience (Hebrews 10:1–10). His obedience now erases our disobedience. Our refusals to offer ourselves to God, expressed in our grabbing for ourselves rather than giving to others, are reversed by Jesus' giving of himself to God. By sharing with us his own obedience to the Father, Jesus gives us what we most need: a desire to obey God, a sincere willingness to offer ourselves to him (see 10:14–18). Thus, like Jesus at the Last Supper, the author of the letter speaks of Jesus' death as forming a "new covenant" between God and people (9:15)—a covenant through which God will change our hearts and minds, enabling us to love and obey him (8:8–12; 10:16).

Reflections. At the Last Supper, Jesus instructs his disciples to "do this in remembrance of me" (Luke 22:19). He wishes his followers to continue to celebrate the Passover meal, as a memorial not of the Exodus from Egypt but of the exodus from sin and death through his death and resurrection. After his death and resurrection, the disciples adapted the Passover meal by refocusing its prayers of thanks and petition on Jesus' death and resurrection and on the kingdom he brings. This, in essence, is the Mass.

Although Jesus does not complete the offering of his life until the next day, at the Last Supper he speaks of his body as "given," of his blood as "poured out" (Luke 22:19–20). The meal makes his saving death already present to his disciples. This meal, now in the form of the Mass, continues to bring us into contact with Jesus' offering of himself to God. Through the priest, Jesus declares of the bread, "This is my body, which is given for you," and of the wine, "This cup that is poured out for you is the new covenant in my blood" (Luke 22:19–20). Just as the bread and wine become his body and blood, the death by which he gave his body and poured out his blood also becomes present. It is no exaggeration to say that celebration of the Mass *is* Jesus' sacrifice of himself on Golgotha.

The Mass, however, does not *repeat* Jesus' death. Jesus offered himself to the Father "once for all" (Hebrews 9:26). His death is the unique, final, and eternal offering. To our time-bound minds, Jesus' death may seem to be only a past event. But his sacrificial death abides forever in him. He offers himself eternally to the Father. When we celebrate the Mass, we enter this eternal reality. Jesus leads us once again on the exodus from sin and death into the new covenant with God. Jesus' perfect obedience to the Father overcomes our refusals to surrender ourselves to God's purposes. His complete self-giving to the Father cleanses our minds and hearts from our sins ("dead works"—Hebrews 9:14).

In a sense, Jesus is *the* celebrant of the Mass. He is the one priest able to enter God's presence and present the perfect offering—himself. Yet Jesus invites us to share in his offering, to join him in his offering of himself in obedience, love, and trust. By accepting his invitation, we regain the role we were created to play as thinking, feeling, loving creatures in this world. God created us to offer ourselves to him in obedience and love, with thanks and praise for all creation. We abandoned our role, preferring sin. But in the Mass, by sharing in Jesus' offering of himself to God, we stand again in our intended place, looking into the face of God and offering him ourselves with gratitude and wonder, confidence and love.

Questions for Reflection and Discussion

45 minutes
Choose questions according to your interest and time.

1 At the covenant-making ceremony in Sinai, the Israelites commit themselves to faithfully carry out all of God's instructions (Exodus 24:3, 7). But while they are still in Sinai, God provides them with a means for receiving his forgiveness every year (Leviticus 16). Putting the two passages together, what do they say about the people? about God?

2 Affirming their commitment to live according to God's instructions was an essential part of the Israelites' entering into the covenant with God (Exodus 24:3, 7). How important is it for us to make this affirmation when we celebrate the Mass?

3 What does it mean to offer oneself to God?

4 What do you bring to God when you come to Mass? Are there things you find difficult to turn over to God? one particular thing you could focus on?

5 In the Mass we offer ourselves to God through Jesus' perfect self-offering. What does it mean in practical terms in your life to be someone who belongs to God?

6 For personal reflection: Where do you experience the greatest need for God's forgiveness and transforming power? Do you bring this area of your life to Jesus in the sacrament of reconciliation? Do you offer it to God at Mass?

7 **Focus Question.** Jesus' suffering on the cross shows that offering oneself to God is not always easy. What kinds of resistance to giving oneself fully to God do people encounter today, inside themselves and from outside? What price must people sometimes pay for offering themselves more fully to God?

Prayer to Close

10 minutes
Use this approach—or create your own!

♦ Pray together this prayer by
Venerable Charles de Foucauld.
Pause for silent reflection.
Allow a few minutes for any
brief prayers that participants
may wish to express. Close
together with an Our Father.

Father,
I abandon myself into your
   hands; do with me
what you will.
Whatever you may do, I thank
   you:
I am ready for all, I accept all.
Let only your will be done in me,
   and in all your creatures.
I wish no more than this, O
   Lord.

Into your hands I commend my
   soul;
I offer it to you
with all the love of my heart,
for I love you, Lord,
and so need to give myself,
to surrender myself into your
   hands,
without reserve,
and with boundless confidence,
for you are my Father.

A Living Tradition

The Eucharistic Prayer, Climax of All Prayer

This section is a supplement for individual reading.

The central prayer of the Mass is the eucharistic prayer. When we are celebrating the Mass, it is natural to pay attention to the individual parts of this lengthy prayer. But it is helpful to step back and look at the prayer as a whole.

The eucharistic prayer begins with an exchange between priest and people:

"The Lord be with you.

—And also with you.

Lift up your hearts.

—We lift them up to the Lord.

Let us give thanks to the Lord our God.

—It is right to give him thanks and praise."

Acting on this agreement, the priest then proclaims the prayer called the preface, which gives God the thanks and praise that are right for the particular feast or liturgical season.

The preface concludes by sweeping the whole congregation into a majestic song of praise: "Holy, holy, holy Lord, God of power and might . . ." "Holy, holy, holy" is the prayer of creatures before the throne of God (Isaiah 6:1–3), the prayer of heaven (Revelation 4:8—Week 3). As we sing this thrice-holy hymn, we not only proclaim God's transcendent greatness, we also declare our sense of standing already in God's presence, rubbing shoulders with angels and saints (recall Ephesians 2:4–7, Week 1).

After this exultant outburst, the priest resumes the eucharistic prayer (in the Roman rite there are actually several from which he may choose). The prayer touches on God's acts of goodness in creation and salvation, praising God by remembering and recounting, ever so briefly, what he has done for us. The prayer then zeroes in on the central event through which God has shown us his love—the death and resurrection of Jesus. Rather than giving a lengthy account of these events, the prayer highlights the Last Supper, the meal in which Jesus made his saving death present to his disciples and enabled them to grasp what it would accomplish for them. And from the Last Supper, a single moment in particular is recalled: the words Jesus spoke as he shared the bread and wine with his disciples: "This is my body. . . . This is my blood . . ." (Matthew 26:26–28). By these words spoken at the Last Supper, Jesus made his self-offering to the Father present to his disciples and, indeed, made himself present to them as their food and drink. By these same words, spoken in the Mass, he makes his saving death present to us and makes the bread and wine into himself, to be our food and drink for eternal life.

This is a climax indeed! But it is not the end of the eucharistic prayer. Jesus offered himself to the Father for us and for all the world. We now offer him to the Father for ourselves and for all. In one eucharistic prayer, the priest prays: "Father, we now celebrate this memorial of our redemption. We recall Christ's death, his descent among the dead, his resurrection, and his ascension to your right hand; and, looking forward to his coming in glory, we offer you his body and blood, the acceptable sacrifice which brings salvation to the whole world" (Eucharistic Prayer IV, Roman rite).

The eucharistic prayer then expresses the purpose for which Jesus offered himself to the Father. One eucharistic prayer continues: "Lord, may this sacrifice which has made our peace with you, advance the peace and salvation of all the world" (Eucharistic Prayer III, Roman rite). This takes up Jesus' declaration that he would give his life as "a ransom for many" (Mark 10:45).

One eucharistic prayer makes this appeal to God: "Look upon this sacrifice which you have given to your Church; and by your Holy Spirit, gather all who share this one bread and one cup into the one body of Christ, a living sacrifice of praise" (Eucharistic Prayer IV, Roman rite). Compare this appeal with Jesus' prayer at the Last Supper:

"I ask not only on behalf of these, but also on behalf of those who will believe in me through their word, that they may all be one. As you, Father, are in me and I am in you, may they also be in us, so that the world may believe that you have sent me. The glory that you have given me I have given them, so that they may be one, as we are one, I in them and you in me, that they may become completely one, so that the world may know that you have sent me and have loved them even as you have loved me. Father, I desire that those also, whom you have given me, may be with me where I am, to see my glory, which you have given me because you loved me before the foundation of the world.

"Righteous Father, the world does not know you, but I know you; and these know that you have sent me. I made your name known to them, and I will make it known, so that the love with which you have loved me may be in them, and I in them" (John 17:20–26).

Jesus died and rose "so that God may be all in all," St. Paul wrote (1 Corinthians 15:28). In the eucharistic prayer we offer Jesus to the Father, asking God to fulfill this purpose.

Certainly we come to Mass with many needs on our minds. The prayer of the faithful, which follows the Scripture readings and preaching, gives voice to these various needs. In the eucharistic prayer, all these needs are gathered up in Jesus' offering of himself on behalf of all. Through the self-offering of the Son, we ask the Father to grant us everything good. Yet, in this offering, we look beyond our personal situations and view the world, for which Jesus laid down his life, from his perspective. As Jesus did, we submit our understanding of our lives and needs to God; we leave it to God's wisdom to fulfill our desires as he will. We join in longing for what Jesus desires: that his followers would be united to God, that we would all know God's love, that we would be united with one another, that the whole world would come to know God's love, that God's kingdom would come fully into the world, overturning all evil and revealing God's mercy to all.

Finally, the eucharistic prayer rises even above this plea that God's kingdom come and will be done. Looking up into the face of God, the prayer concludes simply with praise. "Through him, with him, in him, in the unity of the Holy Spirit, all glory and honor is yours, almighty Father, for ever and ever." As a people, we ratify all that the priest has spoken on our behalf. "Amen!" Here, truly, is the climax of all prayer.

HAPPY THOSE CALLED TO THIS SUPPER

Questions to Begin

10 minutes
Use a question or two to get warmed up for the reading.

1 Whose house would you like to get invited to for dinner?

2 Who's the best cook you've ever known?

This is the Lamb of God who takes away the sins of the world. Happy are those who are called to his supper.

Preparation for Communion (Roman rite)

The servant/the handmaid of God partakes of the precious, most holy, and most pure body and blood of our Lord, God, and Savior Jesus Christ for the remission of his/her sins and for life everlasting.

Prayer spoken by the priest or deacon to each person receiving Holy Communion (Byzantine rite)

Opening the Bible

10 minutes
*Read the passage aloud. Let individuals take turns reading
paragraphs.*

The Background

The Mass is not only the re-presentation of Jesus' offering of
himself on Golgotha. It is also the re-presenting of his Last Supper
with his disciples. In the Mass, Jesus gives himself anew to the
Father—and to us. Our entering into God's presence in the Mass
reaches fulfillment in Jesus' entering into us in Holy Communion.
The one whom we remember comes to us, and our thanks and
praise take on the accent of intimate love.

Our first reading, from the Gospel of Luke, recounts an incident on the Sunday afternoon of Jesus' resurrection. Our second, from
the Psalms, takes us back, once again, to the temple in Jerusalem in
the period before Christ. Our third reading, from the book of
Revelation, carries us into the future, to the moment when history
comes to an end and God's kingdom fully arrives. All three readings
speak of meals. All shed light on the awesome reality of our sitting at
table with Jesus in the Mass, where he is both the host and the feast.

The Reading: Luke 24:13–35; Psalm 36:1, 4–10; and Revelation 19:6–9

Dining with the Risen Lord

Luke 24:13 Now on that same day two of them were going to a village
called Emmaus, about seven miles from Jerusalem, 14 and talking with
each other about all these things that had happened. 15 While they were
talking and discussing, Jesus himself came near and went with them,
16 but their eyes were kept from recognizing him. 17 And he said to
them, "What are you discussing with each other while you walk along?"

They stood still, looking sad. 18 Then one of them, whose
name was Cleopas, answered him, "Are you the only stranger in
Jerusalem who does not know the things that have taken place
there in these days?"

19 He asked them, "What things?"

They replied, "The things about Jesus of Nazareth, who was a
prophet mighty in deed and word before God and all the people,
20 and how our chief priests and leaders handed him over to be
condemned to death and crucified him. 21 But we had hoped that he

67

was the one to redeem Israel. Yes, and besides all this, it is now the third day since these things took place. 22 Moreover, some women of our group astounded us. They were at the tomb early this morning, 23 and when they did not find his body there, they came back and told us that they had indeed seen a vision of angels who said that he was alive. 24 Some of those who were with us went to the tomb and found it just as the women had said; but they did not see him."

25 Then he said to them, "Oh, how foolish you are, and how slow of heart to believe all that the prophets have declared! 26 Was it not necessary that the Messiah should suffer these things and then enter into his glory?" 27 Then beginning with Moses and all the prophets, he interpreted to them the things about himself in all the scriptures.

28 As they came near the village to which they were going, he walked ahead as if he were going on. 29 But they urged him strongly, saying, "Stay with us, because it is almost evening and the day is now nearly over." So he went in to stay with them.

30 When he was at the table with them, he took bread, blessed and broke it, and gave it to them. 31 Then their eyes were opened, and they recognized him; and he vanished from their sight. 32 They said to each other, "Were not our hearts burning within us while he was talking to us on the road, while he was opening the scriptures to us?"

33 That same hour they got up and returned to Jerusalem; and they found the eleven and their companions gathered together. 34 They were saying, "The Lord has risen indeed, and he has appeared to Simon!" 35 Then they told what had happened on the road, and how he had been made known to them in the breaking of the bread.

Feasting on God's Love

> Psalm 36:1 Transgression speaks to the wicked
>   deep in their hearts;
>   there is no fear of God
>   before their eyes. . . .
> 4 They plot mischief while on their beds;
>   they are set on a way that is not good;
>   they do not reject evil.
>
> 5 Your steadfast love, O LORD, extends to the heavens,
>   your faithfulness to the clouds.

6 Your righteousness is like the mighty mountains,
    your judgments are like the great deep;
    you save humans and animals alike, O LORD.

7 How precious is your steadfast love, O God!
    All people may take refuge in the shadow of your wings.
8 They feast on the abundance of your house,
    and you give them drink from the river of your delights.
9 For with you is the fountain of life;
    in your light we see light.

10 O continue your steadfast love to those who know you,
    and your salvation to the upright of heart!

Sharing the Banquet at the Wedding of the Lamb

Revelation 19:6 Then I heard what seemed to be the voice of a great
multitude, like the sound of many waters and like the sound of
mighty thunderpeals, crying out,
        "Hallelujah!
        For the Lord our God
            the Almighty reigns.
    7 Let us rejoice and exult
        and give him the glory,
        for the marriage of the Lamb has come,
            and his bride has made herself ready;
        8 to her it has been granted to be clothed
            with fine linen, bright and pure"—
for the fine linen is the righteous deeds of the saints.
    9 And the angel said to me, "Write this: Blessed are those who
are invited to the marriage supper of the Lamb."

First Impression

*5 minutes
Briefly mention a question you have about the reading or one
thing in it that surprised, impressed, delighted, or challenged you.
No discussion! Just listen to one another's reactions.*

69

Exploring the Theme

If participants have not read this section already, read it aloud. Otherwise go on to "Questions for Reflection and Discussion."

Luke 24:13–35. During his public life, Jesus traveled from town to town, taking his disciples with him and teaching them as he went. Undoubtedly, he ate many meals with them along the way. Now that he is risen, he is traveling with them again and has resumed his teaching—and his dining—with them.

For a while the two disciples do not recognize Jesus, but this changes when he joins them for the evening meal. As at previous meals—when he miraculously fed thousands on a hillside and ate the Passover on the night before his death—Jesus takes the bread, blesses and breaks it, and gives it to his disciples (24:30; compare 9:16 and 22:19). Perhaps these familiar actions trigger the disciples' recognition of him.

When the pair of disciples return to Jerusalem, they speak of the incident as "the breaking of the bread" (24:35). In Luke's account of the early Church, "the breaking of the bread" is a way of referring to the Lord's Supper, that is, the disciples' adaptation of the Passover meal as the memorial of Jesus, the earliest form of the Mass (see Acts 2:42, 46; 20:7, 11; 27:35). Just as Jesus was "made known" to the two disciples in the breaking of the bread at Emmaus, through this meal he will make himself known to his disciples in every age. At the Last Supper, Jesus had told his disciples, "Do this in remembrance of me" (Luke 22:19). At Emmaus he shows us what will happen when we do.

The disciples want Jesus to stay with them (24:29), and he does. He turns off the road and remains with them for dinner—and does not leave them afterward. Luke does not say that Jesus departed, only that he "vanished from their sight" (24:31). Through our continued celebration of this supper, Jesus will fulfill our desire, also, that he would stay with us, even though he is not visible to our sight.

Jesus asks the disciples rhetorically, "Was it not necessary that the Messiah should suffer these things and then enter into his glory?" (24:26). As he speaks with the disciples, he has already risen from the tomb into the glory of his Father, and it is from his glory that he appears to them. In the Mass, also, Jesus makes himself present to us from his glory with the Father, and draws us into the life with the Father that he enjoys. Through Holy Communion he gives us a foretaste of the glory of heaven (recall Ephesians 2:6—Week 1).

Psalm 36:1, 4–10. The psalmist's poetic marvelings at God's goodness evoke the gift of Jesus in Holy Communion (see also Psalms 65:4; 81:16). God's love is a spring of life-giving water, a feast that nourishes our inner being (36:8–9). In earthly life, the Eucharist is the closest we come to fulfilling our longing for this feast. In bread and wine transformed into himself, the Son of God, who will ultimately satisfy every human hunger, becomes our food and drink. In Holy Communion we are satisfied, yet unsatisfied, for we have not yet come home to God. But Jesus is the nourishment for our journey home.

The psalm singer celebrates God's "steadfast love" and "faithfulness" (36:5). God shows his love and fidelity by defending oppressed people from their exploiters, by disrupting the plans of those who disregard God (36:1, 4). God's "judgments" (36:6) are his saving acts on behalf of the oppressed. When the authors of the Old Testament combine "righteousness" and "judgments" (36:6), they mean social justice. The psalmist is saying that God's concern for social justice is as high as the Himalayas, as deep as the Pacific Ocean. God cares for the weak and poor, supporting them against those who take advantage of them.

It is this God of social justice whom we receive in Holy Communion. To be united with him means embracing his commitment to a just society, expressing his faithfulness and steadfast love to those who need it. The bishops of the United States emphasized this point when they wrote: "Too often . . . the social implications of the Eucharist are ignored or neglected in our daily lives. As the *Catechism of the Catholic Church* insists, 'The Eucharist commits us to the poor. To receive in truth the Body and Blood of Christ given up for us, we must recognize Christ in the poorest'" (*A Place at the Table,* section 1).

Revelation 19:6–9. In the final coming of God's kingdom, life will be restored and fulfilled for all who have responded to God's grace. John envisions this consummation as a wedding.

Where are we in the picture? At one point we are the guests: "Blessed are those who are invited to the marriage supper of the Lamb" (19:9). But then we are also the bride (19:7), that is, the Church. John is not bothered by a little shifting imagery!

As the final festive meal in the Bible, the marriage supper of the Lamb signifies our ultimate life with God. At the Last Supper, Jesus looked forward to this final meal (Luke 22:16). It was so that we might take our places at this meal that he laid down his life. Toward this meal he draws us every time we receive him in Holy Communion.

Reflections. Many Old Testament sacrifices ended with a meal (for example, Exodus 18:12; Leviticus 7:12–15). In general, sacrifices were a way of celebrating—or regaining—peace and intimacy with God. The meal following the offering, in which some of the offered food was eaten, gave the participants an experience of the well-being and joy that flow from being close to God. Not an optional extra, the meal was the conclusion of the sacrifice, expressing the peace and unity toward which the sacrifice was aimed.

The Israelites' covenant-making ceremony about which we read last week seems to have been completed with a meal. After the blood-splashing ceremony, God summoned Moses and other Israelite leaders up the mountain near which the people were camping. "Then Moses and Aaron, Nadab, and Abihu, and seventy of the elders of Israel went up, and they saw the God of Israel. Under his feet there was something like a pavement of sapphire stone, like the very heaven for clearness. God did not lay his hand on the chief men of the people of Israel; also they beheld God, and they ate and drank" (Exodus 24:9–11).

The Last Supper, too, was a sacrificial meal, eaten *before* the sacrifice. "I have eagerly desired to eat this Passover with you," Jesus told his disciples (Luke 22:15). He used the Last Supper to give his disciples not only an understanding but also an experience of the peace and reconciliation that his death would accomplish. He was going to lay down his life so that he might have his disciples close to him, as close as those who share food and conversation in a leisurely meal. He would die so that we might be his friends (John 15:12–15).

What is heaven like? What is eternal life? Not even the greatest saints can give a complete answer to these questions (see 1 Corinthians 15:35–57). Our minds cannot wrap themselves around the reality of the kingdom of God. But in the Last Supper, Jesus has given us a profound image of the kingdom: it will be like sitting at table with him. The book of Revelation enlarges the image: it will be like dining with Jesus at his wedding reception.

In our celebration of the Mass, Jesus gives us an experience of the peace with God that he has made available to us by his sacrificial death. Just as his agonizing death on the cross is truly present in the celebration, so the entire joy of the kingdom of God is present also. In the Mass, Jesus seats us at table with him, speaks the words of thanks and blessing, and changes the bread and wine into himself. When we "eat this bread and drink this cup," we receive him as food and drink. In this mysterious supper, Jesus is both our host and our food. He is our friend, who has given and continues to give himself to us.

In his death, Jesus offered his life in the perfect act of self-giving to the Father. By coming to us in Holy Communion, Jesus enables us to offer ourselves to the Father. Jesus' death was a new exodus, leading us out from sin and death. In Holy Communion, he brings us freedom from the grip of our sins and from the fear of death. By his death, Jesus forged a new bond between us and God. In Holy Communion, Jesus renews his life within us so that the Father and the Spirit can make their home in us. Jesus' death brings forgiveness, atonement, purgation of sins. In Holy Communion, Jesus cleanses our hearts and minds of sin and restores our souls.

Questions for Reflection and Discussion

45 minutes
Choose questions according to your interest and time.

1 The marriage supper of the Lamb (Revelation 19:9) is the final festive meal in the Bible. Was the first meal such a happy one? (Take a look at Genesis 3.)

2 What similarities can you detect between what Jesus does with the disciples in Luke 24:13–30 and what he does at Mass? Are there similarities between the experience of the disciples then and your experience of the Mass?

3 The disciples walking to Emmaus have not accepted the idea that suffering and dying is the path by which the Messiah was to fulfill God's plan. How is a person's participation in the Mass affected by his or her willingness to accept suffering as a means through which God may choose to work?

4 How are receiving Holy Communion and acting for social justice connected in your life? How might you strengthen the connection?

5 The reading from Revelation suggests that the Mass is linked to the wedding banquet of the Lamb at the end of time. What are your thoughts of heaven? How can celebrating the Mass enrich your hope of heaven?

6 What do you do to prepare for Holy Communion? Does anything in this week's readings and discussion suggest some things you could do to deepen your preparation?

7 The meal at Emmaus reveals Jesus' friendship with his disciples. How have you experienced Jesus as your friend?

8 For personal reflection: Ponder the words of Jesus to Margaret of Ypres one day after she received Holy Communion: "See, my daughter, the beautiful union between me and you: come, love me; and let us always remain united in love, and let us never separate again."

9 Focus Question. If the disciples had not offered Jesus hospitality (Luke 24:29), he would not have stayed, there would have been no breaking of the bread, they would not have recognized Jesus. In what way is a spirit of hospitality to others a preparation for welcoming Jesus, both as individuals and as a community?

Prayer to Close

10 minutes
Use this approach—or create your own!

◆ Begin by praying a Hail Mary together. Then pray Psalm 23 together. Pause for silent reflection. Close together with an Our Father.

1 The LORD is my shepherd, I
    shall not want.
2   He makes me lie down in
    green pastures;
he leads me beside still waters;
3   he restores my soul.
He leads me in right paths
   for his name's sake.

4 Even though I walk through the
    darkest valley,
   I fear no evil;
for you are with me;
   your rod and your staff—
   they comfort me.

5 You prepare a table before me
   in the presence of my
    enemies;
you anoint my head with oil;
   my cup overflows.
6 Surely goodness and mercy
    shall follow me
   all the days of my life,
and I shall dwell in the house of
    the LORD
   my whole life long.

Saints in the Making

No Substitute for Desire

This section is a supplement for individual reading.

Caterina Benincasa, an Italian woman better known today as St. Catherine of Siena, lived a short life filled with periods of intense prayer and equally intense activity (she lived from 1347 to 1380). When she was thirty years old, Catherine experienced a series of conversations with God in prayer. She put the conversations into writing in a book called *The Dialogue*. In the following excerpts, God is speaking to Catherine about Holy Communion.

Suppose that there are many who bring candles, one weighing an ounce, others two or six ounces, or a pound, or even more, and light them in a flame. . . . You would judge that he whose candle weighs an ounce has less of the light than he whose candle weighs a pound. Now the same thing happens to those who receive this sacrament. Each one carries his own candle—that is, the holy desire with which he receives this sacrament—. . . and lights it by receiving this sacrament. . . .

   Although you all have one and the same material, in that you are all created to my image and likeness, and, being Christians, possess the light of holy Baptism, each of you may grow in love and virtue by the help of my grace . . . and increase your strength in love . . . by using it. . . . Then you can come with love to receive this sweet and glorious light, which I have given you as food for your service, through my ministers, and you receive this light according to the love and fiery desire with which you approach it. . . .

   O dearest daughter, open well the eye of your intellect and gaze into the abyss of my love, for there is no rational creature whose heart would not melt for love in contemplating and considering, among the other benefits she receives from me, the special gift that she receives in the sacrament. . . .

   See, dearest daughter, in what an excellent state is the soul who receives as she should this bread of life, this food of the angels. By receiving this sacrament she dwells in me and I in her, as the fish in the sea, and the sea in the fish—thus do I dwell in the soul, and the soul in me.

Week 6

GOING OUT WITH A BLESSING

Questions to Begin

10 minutes
Use a question or two to get warmed up for the reading.

1 What kinds of social events do you find it hard to leave?

2 When you count your blessings, where do you begin?

The blessing of the Lord be upon you, through his grace and loving kindness, always, now and ever, and forever.
—Amen.

Dismissal (Byzantine rite)

Go in peace to love and serve the Lord.
—Thanks be to God.

Dismissal (Roman rite)

10 minutes
Read the passage aloud. Let individuals take turns reading paragraphs.

The Background

The word *Mass* comes from the Latin word for *dismissal.* It may seem odd to refer to the whole celebration by its end. Perhaps the dismissal at the end of Mass made a great impression on people because it consisted of a solemn blessing. Whatever the reason, "the Mass" is an appropriate name for the celebration because the entire celebration is a channel of God's blessing to us.

Here we read three excerpts from Scripture that help us reflect on God's blessing. The first reading contains a blessing that Israelite priests prayed over the people at the end of their offerings and worship. As a dismissal blessing, it sums up all they hoped to receive through their worship of God.

The second reading describes an old man in Jerusalem who meets Mary, Joseph, and the infant Jesus. The man realizes that this encounter is God's final blessing on his life.

In our last reading, St. Paul urges us to let the blessing we receive from God flow out into our relationships with other people.

The Reading: Numbers 6:22–27; Luke 2:22–32; and Romans 12:1–21

The Priestly Blessing

Numbers 6:22 The LORD spoke to Moses, saying: 23 Speak to Aaron and his sons, saying, Thus you shall bless the Israelites: You shall say to them,
    24 The LORD bless you and keep you;
    25 the LORD make his face to shine upon you, and be gracious
        to you:
    26 the LORD lift up his countenance upon you, and give you peace.
27 So they shall put my name on the Israelites, and I will bless them.

An Old Man Is Truly Blessed

Luke 2:22 When the time came for their purification according to the law of Moses, they brought him up to Jerusalem to present him to the Lord 23 (as it is written in the law of the Lord, "Every firstborn male shall be designated as holy to the Lord"), 24 and they offered a sacrifice according to what is stated in the law of the Lord, "a pair of turtledoves or two young pigeons."

25 Now there was a man in Jerusalem whose name was Simeon; this man was righteous and devout, looking forward to the consolation of Israel, and the Holy Spirit rested on him. 26 It had been revealed to him by the Holy Spirit that he would not see death before he had seen the Lord's Messiah. 27 Guided by the Spirit, Simeon came into the temple; and when the parents brought in the child Jesus, to do for him what was customary under the law, 28 Simeon took him in his arms and praised God, saying,

29 "Master, now you are dismissing your servant in peace,
according to your word;
30 for my eyes have seen your salvation,
31   which you have prepared in the presence of all peoples,
32 a light for revelation to the Gentiles
and for glory to your people Israel."

Taking Your Blessings to the World

Romans 12:1 I appeal to you therefore, brothers and sisters, by the mercies of God, to present your bodies as a living sacrifice, holy and acceptable to God, which is your spiritual worship. 2 Do not be conformed to this world, but be transformed by the renewing of your minds, so that you may discern what is the will of God—what is good and acceptable and perfect.

3 For by the grace given to me I say to everyone among you not to think of yourself more highly than you ought to think, but to think with sober judgment, each according to the measure of faith that God has assigned. 4 For as in one body we have many members, and not all the members have the same function, 5 so we, who are many, are one body in Christ, and individually we are members one of another. 6 We have gifts that differ according to the grace given to us: prophecy, in proportion to faith; 7 ministry, in ministering; the teacher, in teaching; 8 the exhorter, in exhortation; the giver, in generosity; the leader, in diligence; the compassionate, in cheerfulness.

9 Let love be genuine; hate what is evil, hold fast to what is good; 10 love one another with mutual affection; outdo one another in showing honor. 11 Do not lag in zeal, be ardent in spirit, serve

the Lord. [12] Rejoice in hope, be patient in suffering, persevere in prayer. [13] Contribute to the needs of the saints; extend hospitality to strangers.

[14] Bless those who persecute you; bless and do not curse them. [15] Rejoice with those who rejoice, weep with those who weep. [16] Live in harmony with one another; do not be haughty, but associate with the lowly; do not claim to be wiser than you are. [17] Do not repay anyone evil for evil, but take thought for what is noble in the sight of all. [18] If it is possible, so far as it depends on you, live peaceably with all. [19] Beloved, never avenge yourselves, but leave room for the wrath of God; for it is written, "Vengeance is mine, I will repay, says the Lord." [20] No, "if your enemies are hungry, feed them; if they are thirsty, give them something to drink; for by doing this you will heap burning coals on their heads." [21] Do not be overcome by evil, but overcome evil with good.

First Impression

5 minutes
Briefly mention a question you have about the reading or one thing in it that surprised, impressed, delighted, or challenged you. No discussion! Just listen to one another's reactions.

Exploring the Theme

If participants have not read this section already, read it aloud. Otherwise go on to "Questions for Reflection and Discussion."

Numbers 6:22–27. From the beginning of human existence, God's relationship with us has been one of blessing. As soon as God created us, he blessed us (Genesis 1:27–28). As the Genesis account shows, God's blessing is his gift of fertility and the abundance of things that sustain life (see also Genesis 27:27–38). Our reading here, which contains the classic Old Testament blessing, offers further insights into the biblical idea of blessing.

Like the Israelites' ceremonies of covenant making and atonement, the priestly blessing has no inherent power. It is a human action through which God acts—a sacramental rather than a magical act. The priest is simply the channel of God's blessing. *I myself* will bless the people, God declares (see 6:27).

God's instructions to Moses about the blessing (6:23, 27) speak of those who receive the blessing as a group: "the Israelites," "them." But, in the Hebrew text, the blessing itself (6:24–26) uses the singular form of *you*. God blesses us as we stand together as members of his people; yet his blessing has unique meaning for each individual.

The blessing's final word sums up the whole: "peace." The Hebrew word here means security and well-being. And while an earthly state of affairs is envisioned, the blessing points toward a higher good: God's face turned toward us with kindness and love (6:25–26). If we were simply to insert into the blessing an explicit mention of the Trinity ("The Lord, Father, Son, and Holy Spirit, bless you and keep you . . ."), this prayer could stand as a perfect final blessing at Mass.

Luke 2:22–32. Gazing on the face of God is what Simeon is given to do, as he holds the infant Jesus. Although he is probably unaware of the full magnitude of his blessing, he knows that he is looking at the one who brings salvation.

In response to this gift, Simeon praises—literally in the Greek "blesses"—God (2:28). Primarily, it is God who blesses us. In a secondary way, however, we also bless God. To bless God is to acknowledge him as the source of blessing. It is this kind of blessing that Jesus, following Jewish custom, prayed at meals (Luke 9:16; Matthew 26:26; Luke 24:30). That is, he offered a prayer acknowledging God as the provider of the food. In the Mass, we join Jesus in this blessing. At the preparation of the gifts, the priest sets bread and wine—tokens of all God's blessings to us—on the altar and prays, "Blessed are you, Lord, God of all creation. Through your goodness we have this bread to offer, which earth has given and human hands have made. It will become for us the bread of life."

Jesus blessed God in the most radical way at the cross. By accepting death as part of God's plan for him with trust that God would raise him up into new life, Jesus bore witness that God is the giver of life. This was the ultimate act of blessing God. Jesus invites us to join him in this blessing of God also, by living our lives with trust in the Father.

Getting back to Simeon, in his prayer he seems to picture the world as a zone of darkness into which God has begun to shine an intense light. At first, the light is focused on God's people, Israel. But from Israel the light will spread out to the whole world. God's light shines on us in the Mass—and continues to shine on us as the celebration ends and we leave the church. We go out as bearers of his light to the world. We have a responsibility to share the blessings we have received. This is the theme of our third reading.

Romans 12:1–21. Paul does not discuss the Mass in his letter to the Christians in Rome. But his letter helps us connect our celebration of the Mass with our lives after the Mass—with what a pastor friend of mine called "the liturgy after the liturgy."

Paul urges us to "present" ourselves to God as a "living sacrifice" (12:1). As we have seen, this is exactly what we do in the Mass, joining ourselves with Jesus' offering of himself to God. Paul speaks specifically of offering our "bodies." Offering our bodies involves offering our whole life, including our desires, needs, weaknesses, and problems. The Mass reminds us that, in Jesus, we already share the life of heaven. But Jesus has not removed us from the world. Christian life is not about escaping from the world but about bringing the love of heaven to bear within it. By participating in the heavenly worship of God in the Mass, we become better able to face the challenges of living the life of heaven here in our bodies on earth.

Paul does not think that the pagan society of Greece and Rome was entirely wrong about morality and virtue. His exhortation to do "what is noble in the sight of all" (12:17) implies that pagans have an ability to appreciate what is good. Yet people's thinking and behavior are often at odds with the ideals of the kingdom of God as expressed, for example, in Jesus' Sermon on the Mount (Matthew 5–7). At these points of divergence, Paul calls us to choose to live as citizens of God's kingdom.

Faithfulness to God's kingdom is built on confidence that the kingdom is already present among us. Thus Paul says, "Be transformed by the renewing of your minds" (12:2). He wants us to put on the night-vision goggles of faith in order to see God's kingdom growing amid the problems and suffering of the present age.

Paul does not say it, but it seems that we need not only a change of mind but also a change of heart. He sketches a deeply felt way of living, marked by compassion and "cheerfulness" (12:8), sincerity (12:9), "affection" (12:10), eagerness (12:11), joyfulness (12:12), and sympathy (12:15). Such qualities cannot be faked. They can only spring from genuine concern for other people and detachment from our own wants and needs. But how can we develop this love for others and conquest of self-love? Where will our change of thinking and feeling come from? The Mass is our most direct access to God's transforming help. In the Mass we renew our contact with God's kingdom mysteriously present in our midst through Jesus' death and resurrection. This deepens our faith and gives us a truer outlook on life. In the Mass, God fills us anew with his Holy Spirit—the power that can do more in us than we can do for ourselves.

Inner transformation is crucial if we are to discover God's will for our lives (12:2). In order to perceive the direction in which God wishes to lead us, we need to have something of his outlook, something of his desires. Again, the Mass is our chief source of divine help. As we enter into Jesus' self-giving to the Father, we are touched by his love for the Father, by his desire to see the Father's will accomplished.

Paul speaks of life as an act of worship (12:1). For Paul, worshiping God is not simply participating in a ceremony but offering our whole selves to God. Paul's words warn us that our celebration of the Mass is an empty exercise unless it moves us toward worship in the rest of our lives. Ultimately, our song of praise to God is the way we live. Jesus' obedience to God was not a symbolic action performed in a temple but literal obedience to God day by day in Nazareth, in Galilee and Jerusalem, on Golgotha. By uniting us with himself in the Mass, Jesus enables us to offer ourselves to the Father in our own Nazareths and Golgothas.

The Mass also renews our experience of belonging to one another as members of Christ's body. Paul's words encourage us to remember our relationship with one another after Mass (12:3–8). God has given all the members of Christ's body gifts for serving others and advancing the Church's mission. These gifts are as extraordinary as "prophecy" and as ordinary as being a "giver." Whether our gifts are impressive or unimpressive makes no difference: we are responsible to God to use our gifts for the good of other people.

Paul's exhortation in verses 9–21 suggests what a group of believers who celebrate the Mass together should look like. The chief characteristics are humility and love. "Associate with the lowly" (12:16) does not mean to hang out with humble people who are so meek they will never give us any trouble. It means relating to people who seem unimportant or are social misfits. It could also be translated as "give yourselves to lowly tasks"—be willing to take on the unpleasant, inglorious tasks in whatever work you are involved in.

Having received God's blessing, we are to be a source of blessing to others (12:9–10, 13–21), even to those who oppose us or harm us (12:14). Paul's charcoal imagery (12:20) is puzzling. Perhaps he means we should do good to people who are hostile to us in order to spur them to a change of heart. In any case, Paul calls us to love those who treat us as enemies, just as Jesus did to those who condemned and tormented him. It is this very love that we remember in the Mass.

Questions for Reflection and Discussion

45 minutes
Choose questions according to your interest and time.

1 The blessing in Numbers speaks about God's "face" and "countenance" (6:25, 26). What is it about the human face that makes it such a powerful image for God's relationship with us?

2 What blessing do you most often experience through participating in the Mass?

3 Consider the blessing in Numbers 6:22–27 as the expression of the attitude you could take to someone in your life. If you took this approach, what would you change in how you relate to that person?

4 Notice the references to the Holy Spirit's presence with Simeon (Luke 2:25–27). What does this suggest about the role of the Spirit in helping a person recognize Jesus' presence? How can a person deepen their relationship with the Holy Spirit?

5 Some Byzantine Catholics sing Simeon's prayer after the conclusion of the Mass. Read the blessing aloud, and discuss why this makes a fitting conclusion to the Mass.

6 Reread Romans 12:21. Is there some situation in your life where evil threatens? How could you overcome it with good?

7 Look again at Romans 12:9–12. Does anything here point to a situation in your life? What is God saying to you about it?

8 Have the Scripture readings and discussions of the last six weeks led you to see anything in the Mass differently than you did before? to enter more deeply into some aspect of the Mass?

9 **Focus Question.** Celebrating the Mass reminds us that we are members of the body of Christ. What kind of relationship do you have with the people with whom you celebrate the Mass? How many of them do you know? How well do you know them? How could you deepen your relationship with them? How will your life be different this week because you belong to the body of Christ? What is one thing you could do to help your local Christian community become more like Romans 12:9–21?

Prayer to Close

10 minutes
Use this approach—or create your own!

♦ Pray together the following prayers, which are prayed after Communion in the Byzantine liturgy. End with an Our Father.

May our lips be filled with your praise, O Lord, so that we may sing of your glory, for you have deemed us worthy to partake of your holy, divine, immortal, and life-creating mysteries. Keep us in your holiness, so that all the day long we may live according to your truth. Alleluia, alleluia, alleluia!

We give thanks to you, O Master, lover of mankind, benefactor of our souls, that this day you have deemed us worthy of your heavenly and immortal mysteries. Make straight our path, confirm us in our fear of you, guard our life, make firm our steps, through the prayers and intercession of the glorious Mother of God and ever-Virgin Mary and of all your saints.

A Living Tradition

The Eucharist outside the Eucharist

This section is a supplement for individual reading.

The Mass ends, but Christ remains among us. His presence is not confined to the Mass; on the contrary, the Mass renews our faith that he is with us always. Jesus' presence takes many forms: his word, his Spirit, his Church, which is his body in the world. One form of his presence emerges from the Mass: the bread and wine transformed into himself—the "Blessed Sacrament."

If Jesus used the bread and the wine in the Mass simply as a means of relating to us during the celebration, these items would be nothing more after the celebration than they were before. But Jesus' words, spoken by the priest in the eucharistic prayer, "this is my body . . . this is my blood" (Matthew 26:26, 28), treat the bread and wine as more than a transitory vehicle of Jesus' presence. Admittedly, to all appearances the bread and wine continue to be bread and wine. In fact, for that very reason they are fitting symbols of the kind of gift that Jesus makes of himself: he comes to us as our *food.* But if we take his Last Supper words seriously, the appearances no longer correspond to reality. In this bread and wine, Jesus' presence is so real, his gift of himself so complete, that the bread and wine cease to be bread and wine and become, in reality, Jesus, the risen Lord.

This transformation is unparalleled. While we can state it in simple terms, it stands apart from anything else we experience in this world. Indeed, it may seem self-contradictory. Does it make sense to say that bread is not bread, wine is not wine? Theologians have worked hard to find a formula to express the transformation in a way that avoids self-contradiction. The philosophical term that medieval theologians such as St. Thomas Aquinas developed to meet this challenge—*transubstantiation*—states the transformation in a way that shows it is not logically absurd, without trying to remove the mystery of it. But, like some other famous formulas (consider $E = mc^2$), the term *transubstantiation* is helpful mainly to those who invest the effort necessary to understand its technical meaning.

The upshot, however, is that when the Mass ends, Jesus' presence in the Blessed Sacrament continues.

From earliest times, Christians have treated this continuing presence of the Lord as a great blessing. According to a second-century Christian in Rome named Justin, after celebrating the Lord's Supper, participants took portions of the sacrament to fellow Christians who were absent, probably because of work or sickness. Until about the year 300, Christians were not able to build churches (Christianity was illegal everywhere), so they had to take home any portions of the sacrament remaining at the end of their celebration. Shortly after the year 200, another Christian in Rome, Hippolytus, instructed fellow Christians to carefully set the sacrament aside at home and eat it reverently during the week.

Once Christianity became legal in the Roman Empire and Christians could build churches, the practice developed of keeping some of the Blessed Sacrament in church so that it was available to be taken to anyone who was dying. This use of the Blessed Sacrament for the dying is called *viaticum*—a Latin word meaning "provision for a journey," in this case, the journey into eternity. Availability of viaticum is still the primary reason the Blessed Sacrament is kept in every Catholic church.

During the Middle Ages in Western Europe, the Blessed Sacrament in church became a focus of veneration. First monks and nuns, then laypeople began to make a point of praying to Christ in the Blessed Sacrament. For example, around the year 1200, an English Christian (name unknown) gave this advice to women wishing to devote themselves to prayer:

When you are quite ready, sprinkle yourself with holy water . . . and turn your thoughts to the Body and precious Blood of God on the high altar and fall on your knees toward Him with these greetings: Hail, author of our creation! Hail, price of our redemption! Hail, viaticum of our journey! Hail, reward of our hope! Hail, consolation of our time of waiting! Be Thou our joy, who art to be our reward; let our glory be in Thee throughout all ages for ever. O Lord, be always with us, take away the dark night, wash away all our sin, give us Thy holy relief.

Medieval Christians felt a growing sense of awe and wonder at Jesus' presence in the Blessed Sacrament and developed new modes of prayer focused on it. The custom developed of carrying the sacrament through the streets in an annual procession—the origin of the Feast of the Body and Blood of Christ celebrated today. Priests began to bring the sacrament out into view on the altar for periods of adoration and to hold the sacrament in front of the people in an act of blessing, called Benediction. In the sixteenth century, the practice developed of bringing the Blessed Sacrament out into view on the altar for forty hours. During these hours parishioners would take turns praying before it. The number of hours matched the time that Jesus was thought to have spent in the tomb before his resurrection and reflected his forty days of prayer and fasting before the start of his public life.

Countless Catholics find Jesus' presence in the Blessed Sacrament the focal point of their prayer and go out of their way to pray before the sacrament in church. The Vatican office dealing with liturgical matters, the Congregation for Divine Worship, speaks warmly of this practice of eucharistic adoration. "The same piety which moves the faithful to eucharistic adoration attracts them to a deeper participation in the paschal mystery. It makes them respond gratefully to the gifts of Christ who by his humanity continues to pour divine life upon the members of his body. Living with Christ the Lord, they achieve a close familiarity with him and in his presence pour out their hearts for themselves and for those dear to them; they pray for peace and for the salvation of the world."

The Vatican's statement points to an important aspect of worship of Jesus in the Blessed Sacrament: the sacrament remains connected with the Mass. "When the faithful honor Christ present in the sacrament, they should remember that this presence is derived from the sacrifice and is directed toward sacramental and spiritual communion." To draw near to Jesus in the Blessed Sacrament is to be led more deeply into participating in his death and resurrection in the celebration of the Mass.

Suggestions for Bible Discussion Groups

Like a camping trip, a Bible discussion group works best if you agree on where you're going and how you intend to get there. Many groups use their first meeting to talk over such questions. Here is a checklist of issues, with bits of advice from people who have experience in Bible discussions. (A planning discussion will go more smoothly if the leaders have thought through the following issues beforehand.)

Agree on your purpose. Are you getting together to gain wisdom and direction for your lives? to finally get acquainted with the Bible? to support one another in following Christ? to encourage those who are exploring—or reexploring—the Church? for other reasons?

Agree on attitudes. For example: "We're all beginners here." "We're here to help each other understand and respond to God's word." "We're not here to offer counseling or direction to each other." "We want to read Scripture prayerfully." What do you wish to emphasize? Make it explicit!

Agree on ground rules. Barbara J. Fleischer, in her useful book *Facilitating for Growth*, recommends that a group clearly state its approach to the following:

- *Preparation.* Do we agree to read the material and prepare the questions before each meeting?
- *Attendance.* What kind of priority will we give to our meetings?
- *Self-revelation.* Are we willing to gradually help the others in the group get to know us—our weaknesses as well as our strengths, our needs as well as our gifts?
- *Listening.* Will we commit ourselves to listen to each other?
- *Confidentiality.* Will we keep everything that is shared *with* the group *in* the group?
- *Discretion.* Will we refrain from sharing about the faults and sins of people outside the group?
- *Encouragement and support.* Will we give as well as receive?
- *Participation.* Will we give each person time and opportunity to make a contribution?

You could probably take a pen and draw a circle around *listening* and *confidentiality*. Those two points are especially important.

The following items could be added to Fleischer's list:

♦ *Relationship with parish.* Is our group part of the adult faith formation program? independent but operating with the express approval of the pastor? not a parish-based group?

♦ *New members.* Will we let new members join us once we have begun the six weeks of discussions?

Agree on housekeeping.

♦ *When will we meet?*

♦ *How often will we meet?* Weekly or every other week is best if you can manage it. William Riley remarks, "Meetings once a month are too distant from each other for the threads of the last session not to be lost" *(The Bible Study Group: An Owner's Manual).*

♦ *How long will each meeting run?*

♦ *Where will we meet?*

♦ *Is any setup needed?* Christine Dodd writes that "the problem with meeting in a place like a church hall is that it can be very soul-destroying" given the cold, impersonal feel of many church facilities. If you have to meet in a church facility, Dodd recommends doing something to make the area homey *(Making Scripture Work).*

♦ *Who will host the meetings?* Leaders and hosts are not necessarily the same people.

♦ *Will we have refreshments?* Who will provide them? Don Cousins and Judson Poling make this recommendation: "Serve refreshments if you like, but save snacks and other foods for the end of the meeting to minimize distractions" *(Leader's Guide 1).*

♦ *What about child care?* Most experienced leaders of Bible discussion groups discourage bringing infants or other children to adult Bible discussions.

Agree on leadership. You need someone to facilitate—to keep the discussion on track, to see that everyone has a chance to speak, to help the group stay on schedule. Rena Duff, editor of the newsletter *Sharing God's Word Today,* recommends having two or three people take turns leading the discussions.

It's okay if the leader is not an expert on the Bible. You have this Six Weeks book as a guide, and if questions come up that no one can answer, you can delegate a participant to do a little research between meetings. Perhaps someone on the pastoral staff of your parish could offer advice. Or help may be available from your diocesan catechetical office or a local Catholic college or seminary.

It's important for the leader to set an example of listening, to draw out the quieter members (and occasionally restrain the more vocal ones), to move the group on when it gets stuck, to get the group back on track when the discussion moves away from the topic, and to restate and summarize what the group is accomplishing. Sometimes the leader needs to remind the members of their agreements. An effective group leader is enthusiastic about the topic and the discussions, sets an example of learning from others and of using resources for growing in understanding.

As a discussion group matures, other members of the group will increasingly share in doing all these things on their own initiative.

Bible discussion is an opportunity to experience the fulfillment of Jesus' promise "Where two or three are gathered in my name, I am there among them" (Matthew 18:20). Put your discussion group in Jesus' hands. Pray for the guidance of the Spirit. And have a great time exploring God's word together!

You can use this booklet just as well for individual study as for group discussion. While discussing the Bible with other people can be a rich experience, there are advantages to individual reading. For example:

◆ You can focus on the points that interest you most.
◆ You can go at your own pace.
◆ You can be completely relaxed and unashamedly honest in your answers to all the questions, since you don't have to share them with anyone!

My suggestions for using this booklet on your own are these:

◆ Don't skip "Questions to Begin" or "First Impression."
◆ Take your time on "Questions for Reflection and Discussion." While a group will probably not have enough time to work on all the questions, you can allow yourself the time to consider all of them if you are using the booklet by yourself.
◆ After reading "Exploring the Theme," go back and reread the Scripture text before doing the "Questions for Reflection and Discussion."
◆ Take the time to look up all the parenthetical Scripture references.
◆ Read additional sections of Scripture related to the excerpts in this book. For example, read the portions of Scripture that come before and after the sections that form the readings in this Six Weeks book. You will understand the readings better by viewing them in context in the Bible.
◆ Since you control the pace, give yourself plenty of opportunities to reflect on the meaning of the Scripture passages for you. Let your reading be an opportunity for these words to become God's words to you.

Bibles

The following editions of the Bible contain the full set of biblical books recognized by the Catholic Church, along with a great deal of useful explanatory material:

◆ The Catholic Study Bible (Oxford University Press), which uses the text of the New American Bible
◆ The Catholic Bible: Personal Study Edition (Oxford University Press), which also uses the text of the New American Bible
◆ The New Jerusalem Bible, the regular (not the reader's) edition (Doubleday)

Books, Web Sites, and Other Resources

For further exploration of the Mass, see the *Catechism of the Catholic Church.* The following sections are directly relevant:

◆ The Liturgy—Work of the Holy Trinity (sections 1077–1112)
◆ The Paschal Mystery in the Church's Sacraments (sections 1113–1134)
◆ Celebrating the Church's Liturgy (sections 1136–1199)
◆ The Sacrament of the Eucharist (sections 1322–1419)
    Also, on the various rites of the Catholic Church, see sections 1200–1203.

How has Scripture had an impact on your life? Was this booklet helpful to you in your study of the Bible? Please send comments, suggestions, and personal experiences to Kevin Perrotta, General Editor, Trade Editorial Department, Loyola Press, 3441 N. Ashland Ave., Chicago, IL 60657.